The
Modern-Day
Druidess

To Marion

Happy Birthday
2004

love
Chris xx

The Modern-Day Druidess

A Practical Guide to *Nature Spirituality*

Cassandra Eason

PIATKUS

None of the material in this book is taken from any Druid organisation, their books or teachings. It does not claim to express the views of any particular organisation or its representatives.

© 2003 Cassandra Eason

First published in 2003 by
Judy Piatkus (Publishers) Ltd
5 Windmill Street, London W1P 1HF

The moral right of the author has been asserted

A catalogue record for this book is available from the British Library

ISBN 0 7499 2407 1

Edited by Carol Franklin

Typeset by Phoenix Photosetting, Chatham, Kent
Printed and bound in Great Britain by
Antony Rowe Ltd, Chippenham, Wilts

Contents

Introduction: the Way of the Druidess   1

1. Beginning Work as a Druidess   10
2. Creating a Sacred Grove   20
3. Creating a Sacred Circle   40
4. Working with the Sun   61
5. Working with the Moon   75
6. Oracles and Divination   90
7. Becoming a Tree Mother   103
8. Herbal Healing   120
9. Using the Power of Animals   138
10. Working with the Wise Ancestors   148
11. Working with the Celtic Deities   156
12. The Druidic Year   168
13. Becoming a Druidess: the Next Stage   185

Appendix – Significant Dates in Druidry   195
Further Reading   199
Resources   202
Index   207

Introduction: the Way of the Druidess

If you've ever hugged a tree and felt the sap rising, run barefoot through a park or along a shore in the spring sunshine, heard words in rustling leaves on a windy day or looked for fire fairies in the embers of a bonfire, you are a Druidess in her most essential form. For Druidesses are women who love nature and live by her laws. They may work and live in towns, but at heart they respond to the ancient rhythms of nature that are as old as time itself.

The Druidry in this book is relevant to your everyday world, but it will also take you beyond it to experience understanding, joy and wisdom that will make every day, no matter how mundane in material terms, special and touched with blessings.

What is Druidry?

Druidry is a form of nature spirituality that was originally practised under the Celts in Britain, France and other parts of Western Europe during the first century BC and the first century AD. The Druids and Druidesses were the priests, judges, healers and magicians of the Celtic people, and held high rank in the Celtic world. Druids and Druidesses were, it seems, chosen at a young age for their special psychic and spiritual qualities, and their training continued for nineteen years.

Factual knowledge about Druidry in these early times is limited, coming from contemporary Greek and Roman writers who were hostile to Druidry, and from accounts of Celtic spirituality written hundreds of years later, usually by Christian monks who put their own interpretations on the myths.

The Romans, who saw the Druids and Druidesses as a threat to their own political power, suppressed their spiritual practices, but in lands that remained Celtic, such as Ireland, Druidry continued into the fifth or even sixth centuries, merging into Celtic Christianity.

Druidry enjoyed a revival in Britain during the eighteenth century. More recently, since the 1960s, it has been part of the search for alternative spirituality and has taken its place alongside witchcraft and other pagan nature faiths as an antidote to the modern, frantic material world. It recognises not only a supreme creative power but also divinity present in every life form, including rocks and crystals.

Unlike some other forms of modern alternative religion, modern Druidry embraces Christians as well as pagans with its gentle, loving formulas for living. It is predominantly a religion that centres on the life-giving power of the Sun and its seasons, and many of the rituals are practised in the *eye of the Sun.* By contrast, most forms of witchcraft, its sister spirituality, follow lunar rhythms. Above all Druidry is the spirituality of the open air, having no marble temples with statues or elaborate altars, but working with the flowers, trees and herbs in ritual within temples of trees.

Universal Spirituality

Rather than being an organised religion, Druidry offers a personal individual life path that can become part of a modern urban existence as easily as a rural life. It connects us instinctively to the life-giving energies of the earth beneath the pavements, and the sky above the highest office or apartment block.

Druidry has the same reverence for the ancestors, love of nature, and awareness of the life force flowing through plants, insects, animals and humans alike that characterise the indigenous cultures of Africa, the Middle East and Asia. So in a world that daily gets smaller with the advances of technology and faster travel, people of all cultural backgrounds can find kinship within Druidic ritual and celebrations of the passing year.

Women and Druidry

Druidry is a very female-friendly way of life, based on making connections with other people, with animals and with nature in general, and above all flowing with the life force that permeates them all. In its modern form Druidry is primarily a very intuitive kind of spirituality, spontaneous, creative, not bound in its everyday form with formal ritual or the necessity to use complex tools, but drawing for its material and its inspiration from water, wind, fire, sunlight, water and the Earth herself.

Women, too, live harmoniously with the different seasons, their bodies following cycles not dissimilar to those of the Moon, which was also a potent force in the Druidic world.

Connecting with the Ancient Druidesses

You will find a brief general history of Druidry in the Appendix to this book (*see pages 195–8*). However, because this is a book on Druidesses, I think it is important right from the beginning to try to establish a connection with an older Druidess tradition, so that as you work you can understand a little of the shadowy spiritual essences who appear in dreams and in quiet times, and help to set the frantic modern world into an older, slower rhythm. This is not an easy task.

Historians tear their hair out in despair when we modern Druidesses try to find our spiritual Druidess ancestors in books of facts and figures, or by poring over myths. Precise dates are few, names even more scarce, and only the stories survive, but as you work with the chapters of this book you will find the fragments fleshed out and begin to see the Druidesses of old beside you, helping you in your dreams and meditations. For what you will connect with is the idealised archetypal wise Druidess, whom some see as part of our evolved self or as a powerful expression of the well of Druidic wisdom that we can tap into as we learn more of the ways of the green places.

The first glimpse of the shadowy world of the Druidess comes from Gaul (old France). From the *Historia Augusta,* biographies of various emperors, comes the account of Emperor Diocletian, who reigned in AD 284–305. While still a serving soldier, albeit with lofty ambitions, he was told by an innkeeper Druidess in Gaul that he would one day become emperor, once he had slain a powerful boar. She told him that this would be no ordinary boar, but he would understand when it came to pass. Of course, this was a cryptic prophecy, and he did indeed become emperor by killing the praetorian prefect Aper, whose name means boar in Latin, who had assassinated the would-be emperor Numerian.

Groups of nine Druidesses appear in stories from different lands. The Roman Pomponius Mela speaks during the first century AD of nine virgin priestesses living on the island of Sena, the Isle de Sene in Finisterre, who worshipped an unspecified Gallic deity. He described their powers to raise the winds and cause tempests at sea by their incantations, and to shapeshift into any form of creature they wished, as well as their abilities to foretell the future and cure even seemingly incurable illnesses with their magical powers. They were said, with an unusual lack of hostility by the Roman chronicler, to help all who sought their aid.

Tales continued throughout medieval times of the island Druidesses, and local Breton lore dates the last Druidesses leaving the Isle de Sene in 1700 and joining a convent. Even today this area remains relatively isolated and, with its small, winding roads that suddenly end at bays or steep cliffs, or peter out in fields, it is easy to see how it might have been possible for whole communities of pagan priestesses to survive undetected by the outside world for centuries.

Nine Druidesses are also woven into the folklore of the fairytale castle Mont St-Michel, on the borders of Normandy and Brittany. Folklore tells how nine Druidesses lived there until the Benedictine abbey, later a fortress and prison, was built some time around the eleventh century. Official guidebooks record that these Druidesses had magic darts that they threw at the waves to calm tempests.

Other accounts really are cameos, from moss-covered signs at ancient monuments, like the myth of the nine young Druidesses who created special brews in a cauldron at the Pentre Ifan cromlech in Pembrokeshire, Wales. (A cromlech is a huge stone table placed over a burial mound.)

The Modern-day Druidess

During the Druidic revival of the eighteenth, nineteenth and early twentieth centuries, organised Druidry was a male-dominated sect. However, Druidesses today have equal voice and participation in most modern orders and some of the finest Celtic scholars are women.

Although much of what I say does have equal relevance to men, in this book I have suggested mainly work that can be carried out by women alone, with family or friends, or in informal groups, perhaps meeting with a group of Druids and Druidesses on the great festivals that occur at regular intervals during the year (*see pages 168–84*).

Women, especially if they work and have families, tend to have less time for organised group activities than men do, and although there are about thirty-five formal Druid organisations in the UK alone, there may not be one that is local to you (*see pages 202–4*). Moreover, spirituality for women is often a very personal affair, and with Druidry there is a strong direct link between the woman and the natural world. There are core beliefs that I have described in the following chapters but these can, I believe, be best manifest through personal creative ritual. On pages 187–91 I have described how to join a more formal organisation or to set up your own group if you wish.

How I Became a Druidess

From childhood, I have been a Druidess in my heart. My quest began in Druids Heath, a 1960s brick and concrete wilderness – an overspill housing estate on the outskirts of Birmingham where I spent the latter part of my childhood.

Druids Heath is scant on stone circles and sacred groves. But in spite of the builders' aim to raze every possible stalk of greenery, a clump of trees on the wasteland opposite my house flourished, defiantly forming a sanctuary of mystery and magic against an ever-rising tide of cement, litter and broken glass. In this spot I *knew* intuitively that Druids had carried out their rites to greet the Sun, and legend tells that they lit their beacon fires on the hilltop now crowned with towering, barrack-like blocks.

To me, however, it was always the Druidesses who called me. Once, in a junk shop, I had seen a Victorian painting in an old book of a beautiful young Druidess in white and gold, her hood pushed back to reveal cascading hair. She was dancing around a grove of trees on which golden apples grew; she carried a golden sickle threaded with mistletoe, a plant that was called 'the All-healer', according to the inscription. Although she might never have lived except in the vision of the painter, she represented an ideal of the nature priestesses whose love of natural beauty was reflected for me.

I have never been able to find that picture again, although there are other representations of Druidesses. But her image has never left me and I have become aware as I have matured of an older form of that beautiful priestess, browner and more wrinkled, whose robe is less diaphanous, and who has talked to me in sleep and guided me on my path through my life.

I have always loved wild places, rocky shores, forests and mountains, although it took me thirty more years to live in the countryside by the sea. But even though I worked as a teacher, then trained in psychology and became a mother of five children, the call of the distant Druidesses was always there, like messages written on leaves and scattered on my life path. They reminded me in moments of reverie, when waking or falling into sleep, of what I was deep down and what I could be and would be.

I encountered the Druidesses in legends, too, when with my children, I travelled through Brittany in our old, rusting camper van. Here I first heard stories and saw relics of the groups of nine Druidesses who followed the old ways in that area, so remote from the Roman church and central government. I found traces further north in France of folk tales of the wise Arch Druidess who baptised babies at the magical Fountain of Youth in the Arthurian forest, Broceliande near Rennes, ordering fires to be built even at Midsummer so the infants would not get cold.

Now in my early fifties I at last have the time and the confidence to live and work openly as a Druidess. I possess a real sacred grove of trees. The grove is a naturally occurring circle of greenery, the equivalent of a more conventional church or temple, but of course open to the skies. The beauty is that a woman can have her very own private grove for those special moments of quietness and stillness, and merge as part of the landscape into a state of pure harmony.

In my grove, birds and rabbits make their homes, although to others it is only a clump of raggedy trees opposite my caravan in a seaside caravan park with neat plots (except for mine) on a site moving ever closer to the cliff edge as the land erodes. The hedgerow is alive with birds and butterflies and with rabbits sunning themselves, having gorged on my herb pots, while down the steep path is a sandy beach where in the early morning I can draw labyrinths in which to meditate, make wishes on the seventh wave and paddle in the paths of moonlight across the waters.

At weekends, in the holidays and sometimes playing truant in the week, I come to the caravan and live purely by nature, rising with the light and sleeping when it is dark, casting my tree staves made from the twigs of the different trees in the grove and hearing messages in the leaves tossed by the sea breezes that come in from the east.

Like others who have busy lives, I am mainly a solitary Druidess, combining my reverence for nature and recognition of the interconnection and sanctity of all life with the need to earn a living and bring up a family. However, I did make the decision to formalise my private Druidry by training with the international Order of Bards, Ovates and Druids; and now that the children are older I can attend public ceremonies on the festivals and take my younger daughter Miranda, who has the confidence I lacked at her age to explore different aspects of spirituality, joining with others who have followed their own paths to this place.

But best of all I love weaving my own rituals, sometimes with my family or friends but often alone, greeting the Summer Solstice, the Longest Day, making my golden healing Solstice Sun Water (*see pages 62–3*), rising before dawn and watching the Sun dance over the sea. At the Autumn Equinox I try to climb to the top of Glastonbury Tor, or another hilltop associated with the Celts, during sunset, to welcome the coming winter that is just as important as summer in the continuing wheel of seasonal birth, growth, maturity, decline, death and rebirth in nature and in human life.

Using This Book

This is basically a workbook on Druidic beliefs and the Celtic and pre-Celtic background of the tradition.

The different chapters show you how to create your own private grove, and how to work within a sacred circle, using the powers of the Sun and the Moon, trees and water. There are suggestions for ways to connect with the wisdom of the ancestors, personal and other wise teachers, like my shadowy but influential Druidess who has been there since my childhood, waiting for me to be ready (I was a remarkably slow learner).

I have described in each chapter core teachings of contemporary, more formal Druidry, drawn from the entire spectrum of often-divergent Druidic lore and not specifically from my own training order, plus information about a variety of orders and methods of training, if that is the path for you.

Each of the chapters is relatively self-contained, but you may find it helpful to read through Chapters 3 and 4 before embarking on the later chapters. Although I have linked historical and mytho-logical material with practical exercises in Chapters 1 and 2, you may decide to save the historical perspective until you have explored the tradition in a personal way.

Moreover you can read the book during any spare five or ten minutes during the day, perhaps during a lunch break or in the quiet few minutes before your household awakes; it is ideal for dipping into.

Living as a Druidess

You do not need your own acre of woodland to be a Druidess or Druid. There are gardens, balconies, parks, camping grounds and places you can find on days or holidays in the countryside. In winter I use a circle of pot plants to serve as an indoor grove and make the most of every moment of sunshine to go out into the woods.

Druidic spirituality is enriching for family life, steering children away from theme parks and noisy simulated pleasures, to quiet walks where there are trees and local wildlife that can be equally fascinating and certainly far more approachable than the creatures of Jungle World in Florida or wherever.

In the Druidic seasonal celebrations of the turning year you can move away from the commercialisation of the modern festivals and return to the older ways. On Halloween, the Druidic festival of the

New Year and wise ancestors, ban the plastic skeletons and Trick or Treat, bake great-grandma's favourite recipes, get out the old photographs and recall your personal deceased kindred as Druids have done for thousands of years.

Partners, friends and family members will benefit from your increased inner stillness and harmony as you contemplate in your grove and attune to the solar seasons and the cyclical ebbs and flows of Moon times.

The Responsibilities of Being a Druidess

What we take from the cosmos during our studies in terms of acquired wisdom, inner harmony and spiritual enlightenment we must give back in terms of service.

Like the Druids and Druidesses of old, whether you are a solitary practitioner or part of a more organised group, you will have your own tribe of family, friends, acquaintances and colleagues to influence with your wisdom and ability to quell conflict, a power that will increase as you grow in quiet joy and harmony.

As you become more sensitive to the forces of nature, you will become even more concerned about the environment and the well-being of the Earth – the seas, the skies and all its creatures. But because you walk the wise path your contribution will be authoritative and measured, even if you normally fear public speaking or taking the lead.

The Druidry of which I am writing and which I live demands no vows or initiation, except private ones to your own source of goodness and light, or to your own divine core, personal God or Goddess. There are no fees to pay or major changes in lifestyle to make. It is an inner journey and a serious undertaking; the standards demanded are high, based on your own personal integrity and an awareness that we create through what we say or do not say, as well as by what we do or do not do. And that applies as much if you are in your city suit or work overalls as when you are robed or in the special clothes you keep for ritual and meditation.

1

Beginning Work as a Druidess

You are a Druidess if you feel like one in your heart whether you are wearing a city suit or your oldest jeans, because Druidry is above all else an attitude to life. But rituals and special times are a good way of linking your personal spiritual powers with wider cosmic energies and those of the natural world. Therefore I have suggested tools and materials that can mark out certain times and places as significant, and help you to make these times and places separate from the everyday world.

I have devoted the next chapter to working with the most important place of the Druidess, the sacred grove. But as this is a chapter about beginning work, the concept of the sacred grove will be introduced here, so that right from the start you can set up or find this equivalent of a magical altar and temple. It is worth spending time seeking out the right environment, as your grove of trees or green plants will become a sanctuary and a source of strength for a long time to come.

Creating a Personal Living Temple

The living temple of the trees is central to private ritual as well as to collective expressions of worship for Druidesses and Druids.

Whether you work alone, with friends or in a more formal group, a grove of trees or bushes will form the focus for personal cere-monies and healing work, and for rites of passage and to mark the passing of the year for the individual and the group. You can also use groves wherever you find them, whether in urban parks or forest wilderness, for impromptu ceremonies.

Even at work you can create a grove. With subtlety, you can rearrange office plants that may not enclose you but create the outline of a quiet grove in which to work undisturbed or claim a few moments of quiet contemplation.

With practice you will learn to visualise a grove of calm around yourself; it will offer instant sanctuary in the most crowded work-place or noisy city street. Your grove will, over the months and years, become your living altar, temple and sanctuary, whether you live in the countryside or in an apartment block (where you can improvise with tubs of tall green plants).

Finding or Creating Your Grove

Few of us have an acre of woodland attached to our property. But you may have two or three trees, or tall shrubs that have a clearing in the middle, in your garden. If not, it may be worth while, if you have the room, planting small trees or hardy bushes to make a circle; the area inside the circle should be large enough to walk around inside, and to allow you to sit in comfort either alone or with friends.

Evergreens enable you to work throughout the year, shaded from curious neighbours. Visit your local garden centre and you will be amazed at the range of bushes in pots and tiny trees there are for sale; they will enable you to create your grove in miniature, if nec-essary in your living room. You can even buy indoor apple trees, one of the most sacred trees of the Celts. Even on a balcony or patio, or in a conservatory or indoors, you can use large potted shrubs that can be arranged in a circle to form your grove.

In your local park or urban countryside garden, in nearby woods that are constantly being created or restored around modern towns, or on trips to the countryside, you may discover a wooded spot that can become a special place which you can visit when you need to be alone or to carry out spiritual work. In my case, as well as two local forestry plantations of Parkhurst Forest and Firestone Copse, the New Forest with its unspoilt camping grounds and woodland trails is just across the water from the island where I live. As your hidden grove increases in sanctity, so it will attract other spiritually minded people and there will be an increase of flowers, small animals and birds that likewise feel protected there.

Setting Up Your Grove

Here are some tips for setting up your grove.

- If possible, incorporate water in or near your grove, whether a garden pond or a water pump in a large flower urn with water plants. An indoor grove can have a tiny, ready-made water feature or one you make yourself with a small pump, a bowl, water plants and crystals. If you always carry a small dish and bottle of still mineral water with you, you will be able to set up your water source anywhere.

- Weekends away and holidays can be diverted to areas of wilderness, to Forestry Commission chalets or to places of unspoilt beauty. When I lived in urban Reading in Berkshire, I used Dinton Pastures Country Park, an area of greenery where wildlife roamed free within the roar of the M4 motorway corridor; we camped at weekends in Wellington Country Park near Basingstoke, where pine woods gave tranquillity just yards away from the miniature railway and boating lake.

- Holidays abroad can offer a wider perspective to grove work; for example, you may be able to use a circle of palm trees on baking sand or one of mountain pines on a bare stone ridge with the patchwork of the everyday world below.

- Work at different times – dawn, noon, dusk and in the dark – to experience the different energies and fragrances of your grove (*see pages 71–4*). Experiment with the phases of the Moon and again you will discover changing moods, both within yourself and in the trees, the grass and the sky (*see pages 88–9*).

- Experience the different seasons and weathers, such as rain, snow and sunshine, in your grove. The powers will be at their strongest in the days leading up to and immediately after change points in the seasons (*see pages 171–84*). Boots and waterproofs are as essential to the adventurous Druidess as her robe and staff.

• In a site you use regularly, especially in your garden, you may find that certain birds and even small animals come close as you work. You may consider the consumption of herb patches or seed beds by hungry visitors a small price to pay for such contact with the heart of nature.

Your Special Place

As well as having a grove, you may feel the need to have a special place, especially if you share your home with family or flatmates and do not have much privacy.

There are many wonderful tales of Druidesses – wise women in their huts in the forest, administering herb potions or practising divination. Some of these stories were perhaps the product of wishful thinking by Victorians who were fascinated by the idea, if not the reality, of living close to nature. Be creative with your home space and you too can convert a garden shed into your first hut. Wooden chalets are relatively inexpensive to buy from large DIY stores or garden centres and, with the help of those DIY experts among your friends and family, you can be in residence before sunset if you make an early start.

An attic or spare room at the top of the house, cleared of clutter, offers views of greenery out of the window and presents an ideal location to set up a permanent indoor grove and healing shrine. A disused hire or towing caravan can be bought cheaply, and if you have even a small square of hard standing on your property, you can eject the family motorbikes and vehicles and set up camp. Some women, especially mothers, may have problems with prioritising their need for a sanctuary above the children's television room, or discarding the contents of a shed piled high with a partner's bicycles and rusting tools. But plot, plan, measure, declutter and reorder your living space and your hut will somehow materialise, if not now, then a little further down the road of Druidry.

Your Personal Tools

You don't need any complicated tools to aid your progress down the path to Druidry, but you will find the following items useful.

Druidess Robes

You may sometimes want to wear special clothes when you are working in your Druid place or private grove, or when you are taking part in a special ceremony.

Wearing special garments is a way of marking that the time and space in which you wear them are spiritual and Otherworldly. However, dressing up for dressing up's sake is not the road to spirituality.

Classical sources are silent about the physical appearances of Druids and Druidesses. It was not until the revival of interest in the Druids in eighteenth- and nineteenth-century England that highly romanticised representations showed Druids dressed in white garb, sometimes with a gold torque and headdress to indicate high rank. Our knowledge of Druidess dress comes from romanticised paintings such as *The Druidess* by La Roche from the nineteenth century, which depicts her slender and ethereal form holding both a sickle and a sprig of mistletoe. She is standing next to a megalith. The Druidess has long, dark curly hair, and in her classical dress of white she is very beautiful and definitely not windswept or muddy.

You may be disappointed when you see a modern unisex Druid robe, which is quite floppy with a hood, usually white, but sometimes black, perhaps with blue tabards for Bards, green for Ovates and white for Druids, the three grades that some formal orders use to distinguish between different levels of learning.

Some organised groups usually wear informal robes, except on one of the great festivals such as Midsummer, and in winter they wear especially warm clothes at open-air ceremonies. Unlike the ethereal diaphanous robes beloved of glamorous media witches, real Druidesses and Druids tend to be more practically clad.

You can easily make your own robe by adapting a basic long dress or dressing gown pattern. It should be loose with flowing sleeves, and have a hood to keep the wind off. You could use some thick curtain fabric with perhaps green leafy patterns for a long waistcoat or tabard to go over the top of your robe.

If you decide to organise your own group (*see pages 187–9*), settle on a standard washable cream or white crease-proof fabric for all your robes. Your local dressmaker will be happy to run them up if you do not have time or are not a sewing expert. The markets and shops of southern Spain and Africa can be a brilliant source of Druidic garments if you happen to be visiting those areas.

A cloak is useful to keep you warm at open-air ceremonies. It need not be expensive. I have a washable velvet one I bought cut price from Glastonbury, but again they are easy to make. Your cloak should be ankle length so that it does not trail in the mud, and have a strong clasp so that you are not constantly clutching at it as the wind tries to carry it away.

Finding or Making a Staff

A staff is very useful for when you are walking through woodland, for marking out a circle if you want to use one in earth or sand, for holding up your lantern if you are working in the darkness and for directing earth energies upwards through the wood. As you work and walk with it, so it becomes imbued with your personal essence. Combined with the power of tree and earth that already exist within it, your staff forms a heady shaft of the life force when you really think you cannot walk another step up a steep, muddy track, even to find what you have been promised is the most beautiful and sacred site in the known world.

There are many exquisitely designed staffs that you can buy from country fairs, often with animals engraved on the handle (you could find one with your power animal on top – see Chapter 9), or in craft stores in country places, made from local wood. Fortunately, the art of woodcarving is returning, so you may find a local craftsperson who can make you one to order. Traditionally, Druidic staffs are made from yew, ash or hazel, but it is your choice (*see pages 109–119* for suggestions).

I bought my staff at the Witchcraft Museum in Boscastle. It is engraved with ogham staves, the Druid tree alphabet (*see pages 109–119*), and was a lifesaver when I hurt my leg just before the Midwinter Solstice celebrations.

You can, however, easily make a staff yourself – you may even acquire a friendly, resident tree spirit. To do so, find a long, slender branch that tapers at one end. If it is slightly pointed at the bottom you can rest it in soft soil for supporting a lantern or your crane bag (*see page 16*). The ideal length is about 1.5 metres; or you may prefer a longer one, a real hermit's staff. Rub the bark until it is quite smooth, then engrave on it any symbols that are personal to you – perhaps an image of your power creature. Then use several coats of clear wood varnish.

The Crane Bag

No Druidess would venture far without her crane bag for collecting natural treasures. The name comes from the bag created by Mannanann mac Lir, Celtic Lord of the Sea, from the skin of a magical crane in which he carried the treasures of Ireland. Myths conflict as to the identity of the original owner of the crane skin. One legend in Irish popular tradition tells that the crane was the maiden Aoife, who was enchanted by a jealous rival for the sea lord's love. Thereafter she lived as a bird in the house of the sea lord until her death two hundred years later.

In another version she was the wife of Mannanann, whom he punished because she gave the alphabet of knowledge to humanity. The treasure the bag held included many magical and mythologically significant items, including a girdle made of a great whale's back, treasures captured from great battles and, quite endearingly, Mannanann's shirt.

Your crane bag can be of any natural fabric, perhaps hessian, cotton or silk, as many modern Druidesses do not like using the skins of animals. It should be large enough to hold a number of twigs, shells, stones, and so on. The floppy embroidered fabric bags with drawstrings that you can find in ethnic stores are ideal.

In the bag you can keep wrapped in a silk cloth any special natural treasures you find, for example acorns or berries from old trees or trees that seem especially magical. You might keep shells from a beach or from under a sacred waterfall; feathers that you found at an ancient site; favourite crystals; a small bottle of water from a holy well or sacred water you made yourself (*see page 44*); a tiny smudge stick (a dried bundle of herbs, such as sage, cedar, rosemary or lavender, that burn well and can be lit to create fragrant smoke in rituals); perhaps a fossil you have made into an amulet; and your divinatory tree staves in a drawstring bag (*see pages 109–119*). In this way you will be ready for an impromptu ritual whenever you go out into the open air.

You may, over the years, collect a number of treasures and so carry different ones in your crane bag at various times, keeping the ones you are not carrying wrapped up and stored in a small wooden box. Get your children involved too – they love foraging for special fossils and stones.

If you wish you can leave the contents of your crane bag open on their silk cloth to the Full Moon, and from dawn to noon perhaps on the longest day of the year; they will absorb power that you can then use for personal empowerment, protection and healing.

Catalogue items with dates so that as you hold each in times of quiet contemplation, you can recall their original setting and the magic of the moment of collection.

You can also have one or two utility items, such as matches, a pen and notepad, and small purses for collecting herbs, leaves, flowers or berries without squashing them.

Keeping a Journal

Although the Celtic Druids could, according to the Romans, read and write in Greek as well as a form of early Gaelic, and crafted ogham script (the tree alphabet) on wooden staves, unfortunately they did not record their religious practices, personal history or mythology. This was because they considered them too sacred to be committed to the written word. Instead they committed to memory hundreds of long poems and stories that were passed on orally, perhaps over hundreds or even thousands of years, and which may have contained in symbolic terms the essence of their beliefs.

A number of these stories and poems have come down to us in translated form from the original Gaelic. Have a look at some of the books I have listed on pages 199–201. In recent years John and Caitlin Matthews have been instrumental in bringing some previously untranslated works of the Celts to the modern world (*see page 200* for one of their books that gives a good entry point into this field).

While still valuing the oral tradition, modern Druidry does accept the value of recording in words and pictures, poetry or story, our experiences, meditations, visualisations, divination, dream-work, healing and those herbs and trees that have personal significance. Unlike the Druids and Druidesses of old we cannot take nineteen years out of our everyday world to commit what we learn to memory, so your journal will be an essential part of your explorations.

If you use a looseleaf folder you can add and rearrange your materials. You may like to keep a special smaller book for more permanent records, perhaps including pressed leaves and dried flowers, and personal initiations and milestones on your journey. You could also have a symbolism workbook, illustrated with drawings, poems and stories woven around the symbols that recur in your dreams and in your studies.

These documents are a very special gift to be shared with friends and family, and with your group if you belong to one. One day they will form part of your heritage to future generations – for as we learn so we can and should teach others. In doing so we will increase our own knowledge and wisdom through others' input and understanding.

Choosing a Power Name

Modern Druids and Druidesses choose special names that they use when practising Druidry. For example, Emma Restall Orr, joint chief of the British Druid Order (*see page 202*), uses the name Bobcat, which she regards as her sacred creature and whose form she takes spiritually in order to absorb its strengths (*see* Chapter 9). Other Druidesses and Druids adopt the name of one of the gods or goddesses (*see pages 161–6*) who seems to embody qualities they admire. Take your time and the right name will come to you. There may be a particular tree or herb, a bird or an animal that you feel offers spiritual kinship, and again you may adopt its name. If you work in a group, you can use your special names when you meet.

About Druidess Rituals

Some people say that Druidesses are the new witches and there is truth in that, for being a Druidess does touch your whole life with magic. However, in Druidess rituals, unlike in the rites of witchcraft, you are not concentrating on building up and releasing power, but on making connection with the forces of nature and divinity and thus initiating slower but permanent positive changes within yourself so that you can influence the world by your thoughts, words and actions.

There is nothing wrong with practising Druidic rituals for personal blessings. However, with each ritual focus also on a blessing for a person, animal or place in need and in anticipation that your own petition may be granted, do something afterwards to help others in a small, practical way. True white witchcraft is also altruistic, but the modern spellbook trend is often more like a shopping list. In contrast, the wise Druidess is always aware that change and improvement begins within and that a good ritual gives that impetus or strength. Druidic ritual also tends to involve fewer tools than witchcraft, and even these will decrease as your personal power increases.

In the next chapter we will use some of the tools you have assembled and begin to work more formally in the sacred grove.

2

Creating a Sacred Grove

The Druids choose the oak to form groves, and they do not perform any religious rites without its foliage.

Pliny the Elder, in *Naturalis Historia*

Walk into a forest or a group of trees in the local park. Play truant and spend a sunny afternoon in a botanical garden or catch a bus to a piece of local urban woodland or a nature reserve. Go alone or with a female friend, your mother, sister, your daughters. On one of the great festivals (such as Midsummer) you can take your lover and make love in the early morning or the twilight. But for now work with pure female energy, the instinctive raw power that can carry you beyond the everyday world to a different plane of joy.

Trees are special in Druidry. I have written on pages 109–119 about the Tree Mothers, the spirits who are believed to live within each tree and who are wise guides especially for women.

The Celts thought that within each tree, and in a grove or circle of trees, the sky, earth and water met; the sky where the branches touched the air, the earth where the roots wriggled deep and the water that rose as sap from the earth and fell as rain, nourishing and giving new vitality to the leaves. A woman is the same, rooted in her home and her need for security. The 'water' is the flowing emotions and inspiration that help her to connect to others and to the natural world, and the 'sky' is the potential she can reach, without leaving behind her essential self. We will work more with these forces in the next chapter.

Some groves pulsate with power in the centre because they are situated on ley lines or ley intersections, the psychic energy lines beneath the earth, and the circle of trees seems to concentrate the energy. You may find one of these quite by chance. Later on I describe how to find or make a permanent grove and also how to use a grove temporarily when you are on holiday or on days out in the countryside. Now we will explore further the possibilities of working within a grove.

Understanding and Recognising Trees

You will need experience of a variety of actual trees if you are to become sensitive to the energies of different species and of individual trees within the species. Although the oak is especially important in Druidry, there are a number of other sacred trees, notably birch, willow, holly, hazel, hawthorn, alder and yew.

Each species of tree is different, not only in size and density, but also in the texture of the bark, the leaves, the fragrance of the leaves, the fruits or berries. Much of your early work in Druidry involves plugging into this rich source of power and wisdom, and you will need to use your fingertips quite as much as your eyes for understanding the essence of trees and not just their external characteristics.

Even people who do not believe in tree spirits *per se* become aware that individual trees of the same species are subtly different and that in a circle of trees there will be one or two against which you will be particularly comfortable sitting, because their vibrations resonate with yours. Such trees spiritually charge your aura, or personal energy field, with their own fluid green essence. In time you will sense slight changes of energies in the individual trees according to the season and the solar and lunar cycles.

Make visits to arboretums, wooded areas and botanical gardens part of your leisure activities. If you have children, they may complain at first when taken away from their latest video game, but before long they will be building tree houses or bivouacs out of fallen branches and identifying wildlife, and will come home calmer and with glowing cheeks. Stressed out friends and partners will likewise benefit from such time out. Many a covert country ranger lurks within the most sophisticated city slicker.

Carry a good tree book so that you can identify different species by their leaves and bark as well as by their overall appearance. Some trees are superficially very similar, so it does take a while to become experienced in telling them apart, especially in winter. Whether or not you become an expert botanist, you will benefit from what the medieval mystic Hildegard von Bingen called *veriditas*, the greening effect, and so the power of the green wood will be within you even if you are visualising your grove while in a concrete square. Carry bird books and binoculars too, as what may appear as an insignificant brown dot may reveal a creature with beautiful plumage and a distinctive call you come to recognise.

Merging with the Essence of a Tree

This exercise is a good way of regularly beginning personal work in a grove, to mark the boundaries with the everyday world.

- Choose any tree in your grove or in woodland. If possible work so that sunlight is filtering through the leaves or visualise this if it is a dull day.

- Walk towards the tree and stand so all your fingers and toes are lightly touching the trunk.

- Draw up the rich, golden energy through your feet and legs to rise through your perineum, your womb or genitals, your navel and the centre of your stomach, up through the centre of your chest and heart to the crown of your head, then down via your throat through your breast bone, and then through your arms and fingers back into the tree. At each of these spots there is a psychic energy centre that is connected to different organs and body parts. For example, the perineum centre, or root chakra, controls the smaller energy centres in the soles of the feet and so draws up power and protection from the earth, especially when you stand barefoot.

- As you work, allow the tree essence to form an image in your mind, perhaps a gnarled old women, a young sprite or an authoritative guardian with antlers formed of branches. You may experience a surge of energy or a gentler flow of light within you. You may hear words from the guardian of the tree, but for many people this more personal connection follows later. Continue creating the circuit with the tree energy until you feel powerful and protected.

- Hug the tree or tie biodegradable ribbons or flowers to its branches in thanks.

- If the tree is still welcoming sit against the trunk for a while, making connection with the forest floor, the essences of the scurrying insects, the song of the birds and passing clouds. In time they will all merge with you as part of the continuing circulation of the life and light force that pervades all forms of existence. Allow yourself to connect with others in the past who sat in this place and dreamed their dreams, hoped or perhaps despaired and were comforted by the trees; send them your blessings and you may be rewarded by a gentle breeze as the dimensions momentarily meet.

- Record any images or words in your journal and try to draw your tree essence.

Grounding Yourself

You can use an actual or visualised grove and a specific tree in it to ground yourself and connect with warm, nurturing Mother Earth whenever you are feeling anxious or angry, or to bring protection to yourself. It is helpful to make the initial connection in a real grove and, if possible, when frustration builds up, find a tree, perhaps in a square near your workplace (a short break from tension can work wonders). Grounding is also a good way of bringing a grove ritual to a close, especially if you have been aware of other dimensions around you.

Exercise for Grounding Yourself

- Stand facing a tree, this time with your hands loosely by your sides, fingers pointing down, legs slightly apart, back straight, muscles relaxed and chin slightly lowered.

- Raise your hands slowly above your head while breathing in to a count of four (one and two and three and four). As you do so visualise small, golden branches coming from the tree, gently twining around and hugging you, so your excess energies and any darkness become insulated and transformed into slower, gentler vibrations.

- With your fingers extended upwards and arms in a curved position inwards, mirroring the shape of your chosen tree, hold the position and hold your breath for a count of two (one and two), seeing the tree slowly withdrawing its branches and the transformed energies flowing gently down the centre of your body towards your feet and fingertips.

- Slowly lower your arms downwards towards the earth while breathing out for a count of four, so that they end up by your sides with your fingers pointing to the earth.

- Pause for a count of two and repeat the cycle twice more, visualising the excess energies continuing to leave you.

- Release any final darkness through your feet into the ground, exhaling the negativity on the out breath. This will flow into the soil, where it will be recycled into positivity.

- Give your tree a hug in thanks.

- If you are working with balcony, patio or workplace plants, give them extra plant food and run a crystal pendulum over the soil anti-clockwise to absorb any negativity that might adversely affect the growth of the plants in a confined space. You can then wash your pendulum under running water and shake it dry in the light.

Creating a Visualised, Personalised Grove

You can visualise a tree or a whole grove of trees in front of you if you cannot leave what you are doing. You may have to spend a number of days over a period of two or three weeks, working for half an hour at a time, to perfect this technique. Each tree has its own strengths, so you can visualise a particular tree or a grove of trees to give you certain qualities you need (*see pages 27–33* for a list of the qualities of various trees).

This can be especially valuable for times when the atmosphere at work becomes tense or you are crammed in a hot train or stuck in a traffic jam. It also works wonders for relieving premenstrual syndrome or menopausal hot flushes, my own current bane, if you can surround yourself with protective greenery. As a bonus, I have found that by visualising my grove when I am in a crowded place or on a long train or plane journey, I seem to be able to lower other people's awareness of my presence. This means I can have peace at times when I am tired and really do not want to talk to anyone.

It is helpful if you can work initially with actual trees to create a rich internal imagery, based not only on sight but also on fragrances and touch. If a tree does not grow in your region, even in a botanical garden, substitute one that suggests similar strengths. Also, mark any trees that you do not know on the list on pages 27–33 and look out for them on visits to botanical gardens or arboretums and on holidays abroad.

I sometimes work in the New Zealand garden in my local botanical garden at Ventnor on the Isle of Wight, where there is a grove of palms, and in the tropical greenhouse there are even more exotic species from the sub-Saharan continent. The Eden Project near Liskeard in Cornwall is a magical place to experience trees, flowers and other plants from around the world. There are also a number of other reconstructed rainforests under glass that you can visit. Alternatively, you could use a well-illustrated tree book or nature video if you want to work with a tree with which you are not familiar.

Take note in your Druidess journal of the names of the trees you essential use and what feelings they invoke, plus any contact with their tree essences. You may encounter trees I have not listed that have different qualities and strengths, and you can add them to your notes.

You can also get a great deal of strength from tree essences and essential oils, although the former are not scented, but created from the true spiritual essence of the flower. Burn the essential oils or put a drop on a handkerchief and place a drop or two of the tree essence on your tongue or in your bath. Indeed, these essences and oils can be a good way of helping you with the visualisation of a tree, as can incense sticks in tree fragrances, for example pine or cedar. (I have listed some of my favourite essence brands on pages 205–6.)

If you are working indoors, play background music of forest sounds or streams or turn on your water feature as you work and close your eyes, in order to recreate your inner glade.

Tree Oracle Cards

As well as visualising these trees as you sit quietly either in the open air or near greenery, you can create a series of oracle cards for the trees whose qualities seem relevant to your life. By writing their names on card, you are creating a set of symbols or psychic triggers that you can use much as you would Tarot cards to discover which of the trees will be most helpful to you at a particular time. Use them in your grove or at your desk at work as a way of allowing your unconscious mind to link with tree energies.

Make up cards a little larger than Tarot cards and leave one side of each blank. On the other side of each card write the name of a tree and if you wish either copy drawings of the leaves or fruits that you find in a good tree book, or download images from the Internet and colour them in. If possible, laminate the cards.

If you are not certain of the strengths you need, shuffle the cards and from a face-down circle of cards choose three that seem right. You can use a crystal pendulum to indicate the choice if you still find it hard to trust your intuition. The pendulum will feel heavy over the correct cards. Set these three cards face up in a circle around you and then visualise the actual trees.

Tree Symbolism

You will meet some of the trees listed here again in Chapter 7, where I look at the power of Druidic trees, so here I have listed the spiritual strengths of trees rather than their mythological or divinatory associations. Bear in mind that trees from different lands can be used to create a grove. You will immediately notice that some I have listed, such as ivy, mistletoe or vine, are not trees at all. However, the Celts included these because the vine grows upwards like a tree, while ivy and mistletoe wind around trees. Ivy and vine also have meanings in the tree divination systems.

Alder   Called the tree of fire. It symbolises firm foundations for any venture, and power to control external forces and factors in your life. It can offer you security in times of uncertainty and the persistence to carry a venture through difficult initial stages.

Almond   Abundance, prosperity and love without limits. Like all nut-bearing trees, the almond promises fertility for any venture and the fruition of dreams, although perhaps not until several months after inception.

Apple   Fertility, health, love and long life. The magical apple tree promises renewed life and strength if you have been feeling tired or have lost your way.

Ash   Expansion of horizons, travel especially by sea, healing, strength and prosperity. As a world tree the ash will increase your authority and powers of leadership, bringing with it, of course, additional responsibility.

Aspen   Communication, eloquence, protection against theft and healing. A tree of great sensitivity, the aspen brings empathy with others that is not without personal pain. It connects you to the heart of another's experience.

Avocado   Desire, and increase of beauty in self or environment. You will be able to create beauty out of ugliness, but will find that you have to become involved in the concerns of your wider environment, as well as creating personal beauty and grace in your life.

Bamboo   Protection, especially of household boundaries and against the negative thoughts of others. You can draw this protection around you and those you love, but must make sure your own thoughts and words are likewise positive.

Banana   Fertility, male potency and prosperity; involves slow ripening of endeavours and so patience for the right time for true power.

Banyan   Luck and optimism. You can welcome sunshine into your life by seeking simple pleasures and enjoying every small moment of happiness.

Bay   Fidelity, marriage and preservation of family and home, and pleasant dreams. By persevering and seeking lasting joy rather than instant excitement, you can bring true harmony to yourself and those you love.

Beech   Knowledge, formal learning and change. You can learn much from being still in the natural world, and by seeking to give your intuitions and inspiration firm foundations.

Birch   Cleansing, health, new beginnings, Goddess magic and protection of the young. You may need either a new approach or to clear the decks and sacrifice what is comfortable and familiar for new growth.

Boxwood   Uncovering hidden treasure, buried talents and the unexpected. A tree for bringing out potential and perhaps fulfilling earlier dreams you had dismissed.

Cedar   Good fortune and fidelity in love, and mature relationships. A very cleansing and healing tree that can take away the fears that stop you from making your own happiness and good fortune.

Cherry   New love, divinatory abilities and fertility. A tree of springtime and so especially useful to younger people for exploring their own capacity for love.

Chestnut/Horse Chestnut   Abundance and expansion of opportunity. A magnificent tree for bold endeavours and ambitions, filled with idealism and nobility.

Coconut   Fertility and motherhood, and the flow of new life and energies; gives protection against all negativity, especially psychic attack. A traditional source of the nourishing life force of the Earth Mother, encouraging nurturing others and in return experiencing the joys of giving.

Cypress   Long life, healing and comfort in sorrow. A good tree for working through loss and what must be mourned for.

Dogwood   Clear focus and determination. A tree that will stand firm against opposition and cheerfully persevere to achieve the desired results.

Elder   Tree of the White Moon Goddess and of female magic; gives ability to see other dimensions and increases clairvoyance. A fairy tree, the elder absorbs personal negativity. It is a good tree for men as well as women to use to explore their magical side and to suspend disbelief in the presence of nature essences.

Elm Quiet sleep, love and giving. The elm itself is under threat in a number of places through disease, but it nevertheless signifies serenity and dignity amid noise and chaos.

Eucalyptus Cleansing and healing. A tree that frees stagnant or blocked energies and helps people to move forward.

Fig Wisdom, creativity and creative ventures, fertility, harmony and balance. A tree filled with personal riches that allows our artistic and inspirational side to blossom.

Fir The tree of Christmas and so a tree of birth, the return of light and new beginnings, the life cycle and also cleansing. A tree of light in the darkness and the promise of future joys even on the darkest of days.

Hawthorn Courage, marking boundaries, purification, protection, male potency (although it is a female tree), and cleansing; a fairy tree. Use this to protect you from scepticism and cynicism in others and to create a personal space away from the demands of others.

Hazel Wisdom, luck, fertility, knowledge and inspiration, justice and divination, especially water magic and dowsing for water and treasure. Use this tree when you face injustice or feel strongly about particular principles, to allow you to resolve matters by using persuasion not force.

Holly Protection especially of the home against all negativity; a tree also for money and material gains. Another tree that thrives on opposition and uses difficulties as a springboard for positive action; a tree that works especially well with animus energies in a woman or in resolving issues with men in your life. Holly is regarded as a male plant, so it exudes assertive, active energies associated with the animus or male aspect of ourselves. In folklore, the Holly was the King of the waning year (from the middle of June until the end of December). His consort and Queen was the Ivy.

Ivy Fidelity, married love and committed relationships; Queen to the Holly. Good for taking risks in terms of deepening trust and love towards another as well as for sorting out issues of the relative importance of self and others to establish loving but clear boundaries; good for women to work with.

Juniper   Protection against all negative forces and purification. One of the best cleansing trees for clearing away bad habits, addictions or emotional luggage from the past.

Larch   Protection, especially against thieves; optimism. A tree that lifts the spirits and triggers the inner protective system we all possess but often do not trust; good especially if you have felt under threat – whether emotionally, psychically or actually – from others at work.

Laurel   Protection from illness, success and realisation of ambition, and winning through in spite of difficulty. A tree that promises that you will achieve more than you hoped or dreamed of if you meet life head on.

Linden   Justice, cooperation with others, partnerships of all kinds and dealing with officialdom. A tree of quiet, unassuming power that shows it is possible for one person to take on a system and win if the cause is just.

Mango   Health, permanence and lasting happiness. This rich fruit tree promises joy year after year if you plant the seeds of that joy now.

Maple   Long life, health of children, fertility, riches of all kinds and pleasure. A good tree if you have lost your confidence in yourself, suggesting you look at all the potential treasure you have in your life that will help you turn the corner.

Mistletoe   Known to the Druids as the all-healer; peace, love and purity, and also fertility and sexual potency, the union of male and female, and protection and good health. A plant to choose if you are near the beginning of your spiritual journey or a relationship that you believe will prove important.

Myrtle   Stable relationships, married love, fertility, youth, peace and money. Another tree of harmony both with others and within yourself that can stabilise an uncertain patch in your personal world.

Norfolk Island Pine   Assurance that you and your family will never suffer poverty; soaring potential; if you seize opportunities, you will succeed.

Oak   King of the waxing year and sacred tree of the Druids; tree of knowledge, power and independence, confidence, prosperity and potency. Like the ash, the oak is a wise Father Tree that represents commitment to a journey of exploration and the attainment of mastery over the emotions.

Olive   Peace and reconciliation, forgiveness, abundance, nourishment, healing and fertility. A healing tree that can mend any sorrow or bitterness and from this reconciliation bring lasting peace in your immediate world and maybe beyond as your peacemaking influences spread.

Orange   Love, abundance, fertility, marriage, luck and money. Increases confidence, self-esteem and self-love as a basis for making positive relationships with others in which you can ask for what you need.

Palm, Date   Fertility, potency, self-renewal, rejuvenation and the revolving life cycle of nature and people. A tree of the sunshine and blue skies that enables you to regenerate your energies and to take steps forward on a new path.

Pear   New life, health, women's matters and fertility; gentle growth, the increase of quiet joy and fulfilment of realistic aims within the near future.

Peach   Marriage and birth, abundance, happiness, fertility, wishes and long life. Another sunshine tree that enables you to unfold your sensuality and sexuality without guilt or shame.

Pine   Symbol of fire and illumination, cleansing, balance, friendship in adversity, knowledge and protection from all negativity. Like the fir, the pine blazes in the darkness, illuminating your path and burning away what holds you from fulfilment.

Poplar, White and Black   The white poplar symbolises money, astral projection, hope, rebirth and divination. The black poplar refers to endings. Together, the black and white poplar move through endings to beginnings, from regrets to healing and from pain to joy.

Redwood   Limitless potential, long-term spiritual growth and clear focus. This tree tells you to aim high and not to doubt your ability to soar, however far off the goal seems.

Rowan/Mountain Ash   Another tree of the White Goddess; brings protection to the home, increases psychic powers, brings healing, and is also good for metal dowsing and astral projection. A magical tree that will keep you safe from all harm and fears, whether of darkness or of the malice of others.

Silver Banksia   Protection, letting go of sorrow, developing a more positive outlook, new growth and positive achievement. A gentle tree that enfolds you in love and reassurance that all shall be well if you just trust and stretch out your hand to life.

Sycamore   Protection and the granting of wishes; increasing influence over others and situations. A tree whose effects are like its fast-rooting spores, meaning that you can have a real influence for the better on any situation if you communicate your feelings and ideas.

Tamarind   Love, especially new love and the rebuilding of trust. A tree of gentle love, especially after sorrow or betrayal, promising kindness and friendship that may deepen into more permanent feelings.

Vine   Rebirth and renewal, joy, ecstasy and fairy magic. It advises you to abandon the inhibitions and prohibitions in your head and seek what will bring you happiness and connection with life.

Walnut   Tree of prophesy, traditionally where witches meet; health, increase of mental powers, fertility and granting of wishes. A tree that promises the gradual unfolding of good things and the revealing of the secrets of psychic powers.

Willow   A Moon tree; intuition, Moon magic, healing, making wishes come true, increasing psychic energies and understanding the emotions of others. Go with the flow of the hour and tap into the underlying emotions of any situation or person to discover the truth; a good tree if your emotions and intuitions are blocked.

White Mangrove   Nurturing self and others, being sensitive, intuitive, caring, balanced and in touch with the pulse of life. Another tree of connection with others and with the wisdom of the natural world; it overcomes any sense of loneliness and alienation.

Yew   Tree of endings, of new coming out of the old, of permanence, of aims that are slow to come to fruition and enduring strengths, of what is of worth and union between two people after difficulty. The yew will allow what is lost to be mourned for, while reminding you what is of worth, and will endure.

Dedicating Your Grove

Initiation is a word that can seem alien in the modern world, involving being immersed in darkness to shed the ego, rites that include taking steps into the unknown, and making promises to follow certain paths and ways of living. A number of Druid groups regard personal dedication as a private matter, although in some public ceremonies, for example that of the British Druid Order, you can join with others in declaring your wish to become a Bard, the first stage of Druidry in some systems, and being blessed (*see pages 192–3*).

Whether you work alone or in a group, you can carry out a simple ritual to dedicate your personal grove as a place of sanctity; in this way you are marking out within the trees and other plants an area apart from everyday activity and demands in which a special part of yourself will develop spiritually.

So, in a sense, you are making a statement to yourself and to the cosmos/source of divinity that you are joining your psyche with the powers of nature and with higher spiritual energies. People who have dedicated their groves and themselves within the sacred space report that they feel more serene, less buffeted by external pressures, more measured and guided from within.

Dedicating your grove is the first major step towards becoming that wise woman, whatever your age, whom I spoke of in the Introduction to this book. If you do form a group or work with friends or family, you can adapt this ceremony to welcoming them to the grove.

Since you carry the grove within you, the dedication can be in the place you will usually work, or you might decide to take a holiday and stay in a forest or near a beach where there is a circle of trees.

Once you have dedicated one grove, you have created a magical inner grove that will empower any place you choose to work in, whether it is an actual setting or one you visualise. If you are working in or under trees be very careful, especially in dry weather, with any candles and smudge material, and keep them in large bowls or buckets filled with sand.

Preparation and Tools You Will Need

Plan the setting and time as you would a special party, perhaps choosing a group of trees in the garden at dawn, a special location you are camping near on holiday or if indoors one among your plants. You could even make a grove created from branches hung with ribbons and bells.

The time of dusk, with scarlet and purple flooding the sky, is potent, or you may prefer to work when it is dark. Although much of Druidry is concerned with light and the Sun, and many seasonal celebrations take place at dawn, I have found that personal or group dedication ceremonies are better in moonlight. On the night of a clear Full Moon your grove will turn silver, offering a ready pathway between the material world and higher spiritual planes.

Once you have chosen your setting and time, proceed as follows.

- Before dedicating your grove, you may wish to have a bath or shower using lavender or rose essential oil and then wear something loose for your ceremony (*see pages 14–15* for suggestions on making a robe).

- In the centre of your grove set a rock or stone, or an unpolished flat chunk of amethyst, rose quartz or calcite crystal, all powerful female energy stones. At home you can use a very low table in unpolished wood as a central focus. Craft fairs or ethnic stores will often yield such items very cheaply, and a good proportion of the profits will usually be passed to the craftsperson. An even more portable surface can be made with a square of thick slate and two bricks to support it.

- If your grove does not have a natural water source, create a temporary pool of water in a crystal fruit bowl (elderly relations or car-boot sales are a rich source of these) and place this in the centre of your rock or table.

- On the rock light a natural beeswax or pure white candle in a deep holder, or place an outdoor garden torch, sunk into a container of sand or soil, in front of the rock.

- To the north of your candle, place a broad-based smudge or incense stick (outdoor garden ones are very solid and have a base you can hold without burning yourself) of sagebrush, cedar, lavender or rosemary. Use a deep container to hold this upright, or use broad sagebrush leaves you can light in a flat, wide ceramic dish. The reason for using Native North American rather than European herbs for smudging is that they tend to be more reliable in ritual. You will need a feather to fan your smudge.

- You will also need spring (or still mineral) water and a small, clear bowl that you can place on or to the left of the rock or the table if you are facing north.

Making Connection

- Sit quietly against a tree in the grove so that you are facing approximately east. Druidesses tend to enter a grove or circle (*see pages 51–3*) from the west, the direction of the Otherworld, and to face the direction of rebirth, the east.

- Spend time connecting with every tree and other plant in the grove, if you wish, getting up from where you are sitting and moving clockwise, touching each one, feeling its individual energies and saying to each Tree Mother or, in the case of younger trees, Sister: 'Greetings Mothers and Sisters of the grove. I ask your blessings on this sacred place.' (Very old trees may even contain Grandmothers.)

- Continue around the circle until you are back at your base tree and bless that.

- If you are sitting, go slowly around the circle again with your eyes, or walk slowly around the circle once more, touching each of the trees to connect with the nature spirits who reside within. Thank them for their presence and promise to protect the grove, and indeed all trees and other plants (not an easy promise to fulfil, but important if our descendants are to find any groves unspoiled).

- You may be rewarded by detecting a faint glow around each tree, a touch as light as gossamer on your shoulder or a sense of peace.

The Ceremony

- Now go to the centre and light your smudge from the candle. Moving directly towards the east, beginning opposite to where you were sitting, walk slowly and deliberately clockwise inside the grove, fanning your smudge with your feather so that the smoke wafts towards the branches or leaves. Say at each tree: 'May there be peace in this place and sanctity. I bless you all, Tree Grandmothers, Mothers and Sisters, and ask that I may be one with you.'

- Then, standing in the centre facing east, smudge yourself by fanning your smudge in clockwise spirals from your feet to the crown of your head and down to the earth again, saying: 'I join my own living, growing energies to the life within this grove. Blessings be and sanctity. I, your Sister and Daughter, greet you.'

- Return the smudge to the centre of the circle and make sure it is burning safely.

- Now raise the small bowl of water and, beginning in the east, sprinkle just one or two drops of water on each tree or plant, saying: 'Grow strong and be nourished by the waters of the Mother that I may draw on your strength and nourishment in this special place.'

- When you have reached your home tree in the west, sit down again facing inwards to the centre of the circle and, placing the bowl before you, make a cup with your fingers and drink a few drops, saying: 'May the waters of the Mother likewise strengthen and nourish me so that I may be a source of power and embodiment of the power of the grove. I ask, as your Sister and your Daughter, for your blessings.'

- Tip away the remaining water at the base of the tree where you are standing and now sit quietly in the light of the candle and the fragrance of the smudge.

- When you are ready, extinguish the candle and smudge (tap it against the ceramic dish or extinguish it in sand).Tidy away, placing any used candles and smudge in a brown paper bag to be disposed of later, or trimming them if they can be reused.

After Your Grove Work

Unlike in magic, you do not need to close your grove because it travels within your heart. But you may like to use a simple chant such as, 'May the grove be open, and forever be unbroken in my heart and in my life,' and you may also wish to slowly touch each of the trees or grove plants as friends, saying, 'Blessings and thanks. As I leave this place I once more ask your protection as I offer mine to the natural world until we meet again.'

Try to spend a short time tending plants, picking up litter, feeding birds or in some small way fulfilling your pledge to care for nature.

Discovering Your Grove Guardian

You may already be aware, as you walk or sit in your grove, of a wise guardian whose shadowy presence protects the trees and the other plants, and who stands close to you as you work, guiding your footsteps with her gentle hand or filling your heart with prophetic words or song, even if you normally are no poet or musician.

There is nothing to be afraid of, for this is not a spectre or spirit who will seek to take over your life. Rather the guardian of the grove will wait to be invited into your spiritual world and will always expect you to make your own decisions.

Most women do have a female guardian and those of us who are desperately seeking connection with the old Druidesses interpret this presence as the essential spirit of some wise Druidess from the past. However you see her, she may first appear during meditation or in dreams to guide you along new paths and then take you home again. Your guide can also help you to access and interpret the universal symbol system or the cosmic memory bank that will aid your divination and help you to make connections between the inner and outer world, as dream or divinatory symbols appear in unexpected places or ways in your everyday life. Your guardian, too, may change as you evolve spiritually.

If you wish to contact your guardian, you can sit quietly, in either a real or a visualised grove, and create the context in which your guide may most naturally appear. Work at a transition point during the day, for example at dusk, at the beginning of the Celtic day, or near dawn. You may find it helpful to visualise a hut in a clearing or a cave near the seashore and your guardian enveloped in a cloak, gathering herbs in a forest clearing or brewing healing potions over an open-air fire. Alternatively, close your eyes or focus on a patch of greenery and allow a figure shrouded in mist to form and the mist gradually to clear.

Approach your guardian in your mind's vision – she may speak to you and you may realise that the voice is one that you have heard before, perhaps in childhood dreams. Your guide may resemble a conventional Druidic white-robed form, or she may be dressed in brown or some quite different garb. Knowledge of what early Druids wore is non-existent, and most impressions were created by early Victorian artists influenced by the nature mysticism revival (*see pages 197–8*). Your guide may even seem to be clothed in leaves, for she may be one of the ancient Tree Mothers who live in trees such as the elder (*see pages 116–17*). The Elder Mother is my personal guide and has helped me to understand a great deal about patience and long-term perspectives. This has done much to curb my natural desire to finish everything and achieve results instantly.

You may create a gesture to contact your guardian for protection or counsel at times when you cannot be in your grove, perhaps touching your brow chakra, or psychic energy centre, just above the area between your eyes. Alternatively, you can create a phrase such as 'Mother/Lady bless and protect' that you can recite in your mind as a mantra when you seek the counsel of your guardian.

On this first meeting, your guardian may have a message for you or you may simply feel a sense of being protected and cared for like a child. Allow the vision to fade when it is the right time, knowing you can connect with your guardian whenever you wish.

Using Your Grove in Your Everyday World

People sometimes ask – and indeed, I used to wonder about this too – what you do in a grove. Why do you need it? Ask a child why he or she makes a treehouse or creates a den in the middle of a clump of bushes, or why as adults we sometimes need to leave work early or cancel a social arrangement and walk alone, perhaps in the rain in a park, a forest or by the sea.

Modern urban Druidesses cannot take off for the woods or the shore every time the world becomes too difficult to deal with, so a grove, whether it is an actual personal place or a place in our mind's vision, can help when we become spaced out or anxious, or need to make decisions.

As you progress, so your grove will instantly appear on a crowded train, in a confrontational meeting or when deadlines become impossible to meet. You will experience stillness and contact the inner pool of harmony that enables you to control your emotions, your words and actions, and no longer be a leaf blowing in the wind.

In the next chapter we will work with the sacred circle, another way of divining and using a magical space for spiritual work.

3

Creating a Sacred Circle

Within your grove or circle of trees is a sacred space. This is the sacred circle like the circle used in witchcraft; practitioners mark out the area for special ceremonies by focusing on its four main directions and imagining different powers concentrated within the four quarters (*see pages 45–8*). They sometimes create this circle within the sacred temple in which they are working to make a protected work space. You can do the same in your temple of trees.

For your everyday rituals you don't need to bother with the idea of a sacred circle or the different directions. Some Druidesses don't work with a sacred circle at all, believing that everywhere is sacred and magical, and to mark the grove out into areas at any time is artificial. However, I would suggest that you read this chapter and for special ceremonies try to work with the equivalent of the witches' magic circle. If it doesn't seem right for you, forget it.

Druidesses, Witches and the Cosmic Circle

It may seem as though the circle of the Druidesses follows the same path as the circle in witchcraft. This is not surprising, since they are sister religions. As I have said, Druidry is being increasingly regarded as the successor to witchcraft. (Indeed, you may be spearheading a new movement, and Druidry books may outnumber spell books in bookshops in a year or so.) But there are differences and they are crucial. I will try to explain what I see them to be. The circle used in both disciplines is the same but its purpose differs. Druidesses are not generally in the business of manipulating energies to bring about an external change in personal circumstance, as many witches are – although true white magic has many laudable aims for peace and protection of the weak.

A number of Druidesses are also witches, combining the two paths of their lives quite naturally, and there are movements to bring the two closer in ritual. I myself work as a solitary white witch as well as a Druidess.

I believe that pure Druidry in circle work, and indeed outside it, is more about bringing about an inner change so that we think, speak and act differently. Ineffective? Science is beginning to understand how the fluttering of a butterfly's wing can affect the movement of the universe. So, if a hundred Druidesses, a thousand, ten thousand, all make their words and actions count because of an inner transformation, that is a lot of Druid power, pumping positive energies into the universe.

Circle Power

The circle represents the interconnectedness and continuity of all forms of life. Women are creatures of the circle and men of straight lines; women have menstrual cycles and they seem to connect instinctively to the ebbs and flows of existence. Men, on the other hand, can run the life race from A to B at top speed and then look puzzled, asking now what?

Some Druidesses believe the circuit of power can be passed in a continuous stream by physically drawing a circle shape within a grove and standing in the circle with others in ritual within the trees, perhaps with linked hands.

Working Beyond the Grove

A circle can also be useful if, for example, you are not carrying out a ritual within a grove of trees, but decide to work close to old standing stones where there may no longer be a recognisable circle, or near single stones or a sacred well. You may sometimes need to define a magical area in which to work on a beach or a grassy plain. Druidesses and Druids sometimes like to work in the eye of the Sun as well as in the shady grove, especially if the ritual is for sending energy to people or places. In these open spaces, light can pour in from the sky as the land and sky meet on the horizon. In this case the circle marks out the ritual area, so that diffuse natural energies can be focused and concentrated. All these locations can offer alternatives to the grove when you want to try exploring different magical energies.

The Four Elements and Druidry

To make more sense of all this, let's start by looking at the four elements of magic that rule the four directions and quarters of the circle.

Plato, the Greek philosopher, who lived around 360 BC, believed that the universe was made from the four elements: Earth, Air, Fire and Water. Right until Elizabethan times, people still believed that our physical nature was influenced by our elemental composition.

It has been suggested in recent Druidry that the Celtic Druids and Druidesses did have access to Greek philosophy, and some have speculated that they used the four elements in their circle work. I do not think that this was the case: during the Revivalist period, partly because of the influx into Druidry of members from magical orders such as the Golden Dawn, which decreased in popularity during the first half of the twentieth century, ceremonial magic (which made use of the four elements) began to influence Druidry. So although I do not think that the four elements were necessarily part of the Celtic work, since Druidry is an evolving tradition and has quite rightly picked up useful methods on its somewhat circuitous route to modern magic, I would recommend using the four elements as a way of working with natural energies.

Psychotherapists such as Jung have confirmed that psychologic-ally the qualities of the various elements are part of our inherent make-up, and so in ritual we can develop our natural elemental strengths and overcome our innate elemental weaknesses. If all this talk of guardians of the four directions, circle casting and elemental correspondences seems alien to your idea of a natural faith, you can simply sit within your grove or stand hand in hand in a circle with friends and ask the blessings of the spirits of the place from wherever they come – and forget the four elements.

I will, however, give you some basic information and suggest ways in which using the four elements and their corresponding directions may enrich your Druidry.

Casting an Elemental Circle

When casting a formal ritual circle for group work you have a number of choices. These do not arise if you are working alone, when you simply cast the circle around the area where you will be working and work within it.

When other people are involved, one method is to cast your circle and welcome people into it, allowing them to find their own places. Alternatively, you can cast a circle around where they are standing, enclosing them. They won't be able to see this part of the ritual but will hear the words. The third choice is to cast the circle just inside the group. In the latter case I have seen a patroller who walks silently around the outside of the circle during the ceremony, like an ancient guard, so that the ceremony will not be disturbed.

The Triple Circle

The triple circle is one of the most ancient and powerful forms of circle casting in both magic and Druidry, as well as offering in your everyday world a powerful source of psychic protection if cast around your home or workspace, or around a drawing representing them. You can also cast a circle around your grove if you are feeling vulnerable or have been subjected to a lot of stress or hostility and find it difficult to focus. Three is a very important number in Druidry, since the Celts believed that there were three realms, Earth, Sea and Sky, and that Fire was the unifying generative/cleansing force behind existence. These realms are not abstract concepts. They are the Earth beneath your feet, the Sky above and the vast oceans that mark the limits of the land. I have written in detail about these realms on pages 54–8, but for now it is the elements that are the main focus.

This circle uses salt for Earth, water for its own element (linked with the realm of the Sea), smoke for Air (linked with the realm of the Air) and optionally a candle or a torch for Fire. The method of working is as follows.

- Create your first circle clockwise with sea salt outside or just within a circle of people or, if you are alone, around your sacred area. If you prefer, different people can cast the different elements. In Druidry you normally begin in the east, but if you follow a more magical tradition you can cast from the north. In either case create a complete clockwise circle; you can use a compass or estimate the four main directions. As I said earlier, Druidic circles tend to be open ones but with a more formal circle you might like to say something along the lines of, 'May this circle of Earth and of protection remain unbroken in our hearts and in our minds whether we are in this place or far away. Blessings be.'

- Then make a second circle clockwise by sprinkling pure mineral water or Sun or Moon water with your fingers from a dish or with a bundle of twigs dipped into the water (*see pages 62–3 and 82–3*). Make the second circle just beyond the first, again beginning in the east or north. As you do so, say, 'May the circle of the Waters and of love remain unbroken in our hearts and in our minds whether we are in this place or far away. Blessings be.'

- Finally create a third clockwise circle using a censer of incense, or a smudge or incense stick of sage, cedar or pine, just outside the circle of water, saying, 'May the circle of the Sky and of power remain unbroken in our hearts and in our minds. Blessings be.'

- If you want to include the fourth element, Fire, sprinkle a few grains of salt into the water, stir it clockwise with a clear quartz crystal and use that for the first circle, adapting the chant to invoke Earth and Water/the Seas. The second circle then becomes Smoke/Air and the third Fire/the Sun. You can carry a torch or large candle around the circle just outside the first two for your Fire. Adding salt to water is one way of making sacred water.

The Properties of the Four Elements

Before we go further in using the elements in circle rituals, I will list the properties of the elements that are relevant to Druid ritual. I have included for each element deities that have become associated with the Celtic world. I find they form a good focus when you are working with the different elements. If you wish you can look up the deities in the list on pages 161–6.

Earth

Earth represents north, midnight and winter.

Colours   Green or brown.

Qualities   Stability, common sense, roundedness, practical abilities, caretaker of the Earth, protectiveness, upholder of tradition, love of beauty, patience and perseverance, generosity, acceptance of others, nurturing powers.

Rules over   Abundance and prosperity, fertility, finance, law and order, institutions, authority, motherhood, the physical body, food, home and family, animals, the land, agriculture, horticulture and environmentalism, womb and tomb.

Celtic deities   The Cailleach are the old crone goddesses of winter who can shape shift into many forms, including trees, hares, cats, standing stones and lovely maidens; they care for the animals in winter and cast down snow to allow the land to rest and be restored. Also the Earth Father Cernunnos/Herne the Hunter, Lord of the Hunt and the Herds and sacrificial God of Winter (*see page 163*).

Crystals   Agates, emerald, jet, obsidian, rose quartz, rutilated quartz, tiger's eye.

Places   Megaliths, stone circles, groves, forests, homes, temples, the crypts of churches and cathedrals that are built over sacred Druidic places, cromlechs, ley lines, caves.

Power animals/birds   Bear, bull, serpent, snake.

Substances and materials   Salt, herbs, flowers, trees, coins, bread, corn and wheat, nuts, clay, grass, soil, sand, berries, pot pourri, cauldrons, dishes.

Air

Air represents the east, dawn and spring.

Colours   Yellow and grey.

Qualities   Logic, clear focus, an enquiring and analytical mind, the ability to communicate clearly, concentration, versatility, adaptability, quest for truth, commercial and technological acumen, healing powers through channelling higher energies.

Rules over   New beginnings, change, health and healing, teaching, travel, house or career moves, knowledge, examinations, the media, science, ideas, ideals, money-spinning.

Celtic deities   Arianrhod, the Welsh Goddess of magical inspiration, the Sky, and the Full Moon, and keeper of the constantly circling Silver Wheel of Stars. Also Taranis, the Thunder God who turns the Wheel of Fate and enables change to occur; he is often pictured rising from a tree (*see page 166*).

Crystals   Amethyst, clear crystal quartz, citrine, diamond, lapis lazuli, sodalite, sugilite, sapphire.

Places   Mountaintops, hills, towers, steeples and spires of churches and cathedrals, the sky, pyramids, open plains, tall buildings, balconies, roof gardens.

Power animals/birds   Eagle, hawk, bird of prey, white dove.

Substances and materials   Four winds, clouds, balloons, kites, swords, knives, feathers, air-borne seeds and spores, incense, smudge sticks, smoke, mist, oils, storms, boats with sails billowing in the wind, weather vanes.

Fire

Fire represents the south, noon and summer.

Colours   Red, orange or gold.

Qualities   Fertility in all aspects of life, creativity, bringing light, power, passion, joy, initiating, transformation, courage.

Rules over   Ambition, achievement, illumination, inspiration, all creative and artistic ventures, poetry, art, sculpture, writing, music, dance, religion and spirituality, psychic powers, especially higher ones such as channelling, innovation, sexuality. It is also potent for destruction of what is now no longer needed, for binding, and for banishing rituals and therefore for protection.

Celtic deities The triple Goddess Brighid is a goddess of Fire and the Sun. She is said in Irish folklore to hang her cloak on the Sun's rays; she is also goddess of the Hearth and patroness of all smiths as well as of healing and poetry. Bel or Belenus is the Shining One, God of Fire who gives his name to the cleansing Beltaine fires at the beginning of May; he was a focus also for the balefires at Samhain at Halloween, when light gave way to darkness (*see pages 173–4*).

Crystals Amber, bloodstone, boji stones, carnelian, garnet, lava, iron pyrites, ruby, topaz, turquoise.

Places Hearths, bonfires, deserts, volcanoes, sacred festival fires, hilltop beacons, all conflagrations, solar eclipses.

Power animals/birds Stag, lion, dragon, ram and the legendary golden phoenix, symbol of transformation and rebirth – the phoenix burned itself on a funeral pyre every five hundred years, and a young phoenix rose golden from the ashes.

Substances and materials Candles, beeswax, flames, ash, fibre-optic lamps, the Sun, lightning, wands, spears and lances, fire, torches, Jack o'lanterns, clear crystal spheres, mirrors, suncatchers, sunflowers and all other golden flowers.

Water

Water represents the west, dusk and autumn.

Colours Blue and silver.

Qualities Empathy, inner harmony, peacemaker, unconscious wisdom, ability to merge and interconnect with nature, the cycles of the seasons, the life cycle.

Rules over Love, relationships, friendship, dreams, purification rites, healing using the powers of nature, especially crystals and sacred water, scrying (seeking images in water), divination, all water and sea magic, Moon magic, travel by sea.

Celtic deities Cerridwen, Goddess of Druidic initiation who brews in her cauldron the elixir of inspiration and rebirth. Mannanann or Manannan mac Lir, Manx God of the Sea who could create storms or bring down mist to protect his people. He is especially associated with islands and headlands as land meets sea;

as a great magician he is also linked with the Other World Isles of the Blest, especially Arran and the Isle of Man.

Crystals Aquamarine, calcite, coral, jade, moonstone, fluorite, pearl, opal, tourmaline.

Places The ocean, rivers, lakes, pools, sacred wells and streams, marshland, flood plains.

Power animals/birds Frog, dolphin, otter and beaver, all fish, especially the salmon.

Symbols and substances Milk, water, blood, sea shells, kelp, wine, cups, chalices.

Walking the Directions

In order to get to know these elemental powers from the inside spend time creating a triple circle and then walking it.

You can move around the perimeter of your circle in ritual. Different rituals and festivals can begin in different places. You might begin a spring ritual in the east; an Earth or winter solstice ritual in the north, its own direction; a summer solstice ritual from the south; or a Water or autumn equinox ritual in the west.

Working in one Druidic tradition you might learn one method, only to find that other groups work differently. Who is right? They all are, so if you are working alone or with your own group, it's fine to experiment.

Weaving the Elements

Since all the elements are part of the same whole, you can work in your circle, weaving the elements into a pattern by walking direct pathways diagonally between the different elements. Note in your journal the combinations that gave you particularly meaningful walks, expressed by a sense of peace, or by significant dreams or divination after the ritual that answer questions you had not realised you needed to ask.

You can work in a cross formation unless elements are next to each other, in which case move in a clockwise direction. Allow your feet to take you to the starting point. This may not be the one you anticipated. Unless you have a strong feeling that you need a particular strength, allow your feet to guide you. Perhaps you could create pathways between the elements on a circle in your garden, using stone pathways to make the interconnections.

The following are connections that may be helpful initially. If in doubt, imagine the effect, for example, of Water on Fire or Air on Fire. This may cast images as you walk, which in turn evoke memories and feelings related to your own life.

- **North to South, Earth to Fire**, for an increase in power, joy and illumination; good if you need a sudden surge of energy to act or clarify matters.

- **South to North, Fire to Earth**, to move from the outer to the inner world, to allow plans and ideas to lie fallow, and to relieve a sense of urgency that is wearing you out rather than achieving results.

- **West to East, Water to Air**, towards the rising light, the direction of rebirth, new beginnings and regeneration after illness or sorrow.

- **East to West, Air to Water**, to reap what has been sown, to lay down old burdens and to allow time to heal.

- **North to East, Earth to Air**, to bring the seeds of plans and dreams into the outer world, and to learn to trust and love again.

- **East to North, Air to Earth**, to move away from malice, destructive situations and relationships, and keep one's own counsel for a while.

- **South to East, Fire to Air**, to increase the impetus for any endeavour, and to seek substance through which to channel dreams and energies.

- **East to South, Air to Fire**, for maximum increase, a natural progression for fulfilling any goals that also demand maximum effort.

- **North to West, Earth to Water**, to seek wisdom from the past, and to reassess mistakes and missed opportunities, and let them go.

- **West to North, Water to Earth**, to let go of the desire for control and to walk trustfully into the darkness, knowing light will return.

- **South to West, Fire to Water**, to allow events to run their course and attain balance in your emotions.

- **West to South, Water to Fire**, to temper anger and desire with altruism and compassion.

You can carry out your elemental walks even without casting a circle by walking around your grove, identifying trees or plants to represent the four quarters. In a grove you may find that your elemental guardians are Tree Mothers or essences, and if you work in the same grove they will help you in your weaving.

Druid Circle Rituals

Preparing your circle for ritual is rather like getting your home ready for special guests. You want the area to be clean and welcoming.

Preparing for Ritual

For special rituals you may want to sweep the area where you are casting the triple circle with psychically cleansing pine or cedar branches, or a bundle of tied ash or hazel twigs that have been dipped in water into which a pinch of salt has been stirred.

If you are working indoors, perhaps in bad weather, with maybe some tubs of greenery for an impromptu grove, you could use just a few drops of spring water, or scatter dried lavender or chamomile flowers within the circle you have made and then sweep them away, taking with them any absorbed negativity, and making the area feel cleansed for casting your magical circle.

Once you have prepared your circle, positive forces of higher energy, called in modern Druidry the Shining Ones, the equivalent of Archangels in conventional magic, will come together. If it is an idea that does not appeal you may visualise these forces of light and protection as pillars or shafts of light.

Working with the Druidess Circle

In this section we return to the differences between Druidry and witchcraft. Druidess circles, even the most formally cast ones, tend to remain open in order to welcome latecomers and allow people to leave quietly. In practice, this works well as long as you make sure you have four earthly Gatekeepers at the four main compass directions, who are there from the beginning and stay to the end to hold the circle energies intact.

Another job of these earthly Gatekeepers is to greet the Shining Ones, the spiritual Gatekeepers of the four directions. These spiritual Gatekeepers protect the edges of the circle so that you can work without worrying about releasing negative energies if you are maybe dealing with a sad issue or doing healing of the Earth.

You and your circle, and maybe a few friends, may not want to worry about these formal symbols of magic and can rely on your Shining Beings to turn up even if you are working alone. Instead of building up energies to release them into the cosmos, as is done in magic, Druidesses absorb those strengths into themselves and also make offerings of flowers or herbs to Mother Earth, and the Shining Ones that are left in the circle.

Sometimes we can leave our weaknesses and sorrows with our offerings, asking that they be absorbed by the Earth and replaced with healing powers.

Marking the Sacred Centre

If you are working alone or with a few friends, make a triple circle of protection within the grove of trees, just large enough to walk around and sit in.

You can mark the sacred centre both for your solitary circle rituals and for those with a group with a table to contain tools, a stone to represent the guardian of the stones or a cauldron. You can cross your circle horizontally and vertically without stepping in the sacred centre. Other Druidesses prefer to leave the centre empty, visualising a small circle of light right in the middle, a doorway through which you can invite the ancestors.

Meeting the Elemental Guardians of the Quarters

Now we need to look at the different powers of the spirit guardians of the four directions, who form doorways of power in formal ritual as well as offering protection. We will start in the east.

- Cast your circle from the east and when it is complete stand in the east, facing outwards. In group rituals different people take on responsibility for calling upon the energies of the four quarters. They can be thought of magically as the guardians of the Earth, Air, Fire and Water, or to put it in more modern terms as personifications or representations of the four different kinds of psychic energy.

- Before you greet the guardian of Air in the east, visualise early morning mist or dawning light ahead, and allow the guardian to form – different places may evoke different elemental guardians. The guardian may be a wise Druidess who lived long ago, a shining being who guides humankind from the Otherworld or a specific deity form, not necessarily one I suggest as being associated with each element.

- Ask yourself what characteristics this guardian of Air will possess. Some or all of those listed on page 46 for the Air element certainly; generally this guardian is quite young, dynamic and may be impatient to be on with the ceremony. Listen to the voice that may appear in the wind and you may understand a little of the guardian's enthusiasm and desire for change, although you may also unwillingly shed a few illusions. When you are ready, welcome the guardian of the east to the ritual and open the portal either by actually creating a clockwise arc or by visualising a doorway of sunrise.

- Move next around your circle to the south and, again facing outwards, look into what may be visualised as brilliant noonday Sun. This guardian will be even more dynamic, surrounded by a halo of light, like flame never still, but shedding inspiration and illumination and lighting those dark corners. When you are ready, welcome this guardian to the circle and open the portal to the south, again by either creating an arc or visualising a doorway of noonday brilliance.

- Move next to the west and look outwards into what may be a glorious sunset or a gentler fading of the light. This guardian will be gentler and speak softly of reconciliation and healing. This is an easy guardian to admit, being kindly, and you may again create an arc with your hand or visualise the door into shadows, but not frightening ones. Although this was the direction of death to the Celts, it was not feared, but was regarded as a return to the womb and then a walk to the east to rise once more with the dawn.

• Finally move to the north and look outwards, not into the void, but into velvety darkness in which shine thousands of stars and the silver wheel of Arianrhod. This guardian will probably be a wise grandfather or a gentle but firm grandmother, encouraging you to step off the frantic wheel of modern life and wait in the stillness, listening to the heart of silence that is said to be more harmonious than the most beautiful sound (T. S. Eliot called it 'the silence between two waves'). Greet this guardian and either create your arc or perhaps see a door opening in the face of the Moon.

• When you close the doorways after a ritual, thank your guardians in turn, either in the order you met them or in the reverse order. Close the door either with an anti-clockwise arc, or by visualising the gateway closing.

What enters the circle when you open the doorways? The answer is the strength and wisdom of each direction for you to absorb, allowing the cosmic forces to infuse you with the specific energies you need.

Inviting the Wise Ancestors Into the Circle

Druidesses sometimes invite the Wise Ancestors (*see* Chapter 10) to join them within the sacred circle. For special rituals you can leave offerings to the Wise Ancestors who keep us safe when we are carrying out rituals, and at other times too.

Wise Ancestors can be described as being like your favourite great grandma, who died when you were young, and whose presence you can sometimes sense or whose perfume you can sometimes smell if you are sad. If this seems unsettling think of people in your family centuries back whose lives you carry in your gènes, and whose stories are told in the family – those pioneer folk who crossed oceans to a new land or, in the case of my ancestors, hitched up a cart with their furniture and came into the town from the countryside in the nineteenth century to find work. You can also focus on spiritual ancestors, maybe those wise, elusive Druidesses or the feisty Celtic women, such as the Queen of the Iceni Boudicca, who took on the Roman army when they raped her daughters and threatened her tribe.

Working with the Three Realms

Another difference between Druidry and witchcraft is that Druidesses also work with the concept of the three realms of Earth, Sea and Sky – a concept that has passed down to us from Revivalist Druidry. This is an excellent way to work with sources of natural power, even if you do not ever use a sacred circle. Indeed, some Druidesses ignore the sacred circle and draw a symbol of the three realms, the three-armed symbol of the triskele (*see pages 58–60*), and use that as a focus for magic power. The beauty of Druidry is that there are so many options; almost everyone, by mixing and matching, comes up with a way of focusing power.

The Earth/Land

This is the natural home of people, animals, insects, plants, trees, crystals and stones, and since it is the realm with which we are most familiar, it may be the easiest one to begin with. However, if you live and work near the sea, or in a community that still depends on fishing, then the Sea may be your natural realm. Fresh water from wells and rivers is sometimes included in the Earth, but I feel it is more naturally included within the Sea realm.

The Land is generally relatively stable, although earthquakes and erosion can bring change. So if the Land beneath our feet can vanish, we should certainly learn to cherish it. Spend a while walking barefoot over earth or grass and digging soil or sand, whether outdoors or in pot plants or a sand tray. Make pots and creatures out of clay; it is only as we grow up that we begin to worry about getting dirty when working with the earth, so that we can lose our natural connection with the Land.

One of the Druidic initiations (according to the more modern accounts at least) involved entering a cave or subterranean chamber beneath a great stone table (a cromlech) and welcoming the darkness. This is psychologically and psychically a powerful method of understanding Earth power. You will gradually get used to dark places if you are gentle with yourself, and this can be an important way of connecting with your inner wisdom and prophetic powers (*see pages 100–102*). Or you can bury yourself partly in sand at the beach on a warm day and wriggle within it.

According to legends and to accounts of people in Celtic lands collected from Victorian times, and by folklorists in the early part of the twentieth century, every place has its land wights, those brown, shadowy, tall guardians who care for the Earth and the places we have built on it. If you want to read more about these accounts you will find them in my *Complete Guide to Fairies and Magical Beings*.

If you leave offerings for them, perhaps a few flowers or a little milk near your boundaries, you will sense their protection. Since they take only the essence, you will need to keep your offerings pot regularly cleansed and fresh. If you live in a block of flats, you can place small offerings of seeds in a plant pot on your windowsill or balcony and watch them thrive. If you work in a place where the atmosphere is bad, place jade or amethyst crystals in the soil of a plant pot to attract the benign spirit of the forgotten guardians.

Becoming a caretaker of the Earth realm is quite onerous. It involves picking up litter, campaigning on environmental issues and above all teaching children – even the tiresome ones next door – the wonders of the Earth, perhaps by allowing them to see your collection of crystals or giving them plants to care for.

The Sea

The Sea is wild and constantly changing, ebbing and flowing, affected by the pull of the Moon as water is sucked up from it into the Sky, being returned in the endless cycle of rain and rivers. It too has a rich life of fish, seals and seabirds, as well as a myriad of plants.

Find water, whether the ocean, a river, lakes or ponds, and watch their changing moods according to the seasons and the weather. Swim or paddle even in a swimming pool and if you are brave

enough immerse yourself in water; another aspect of Druidic
initiation involved standing under a waterfall.

Spend time in your bathroom, lit by scented candles, swirling
the light pools in your bath or recreating a waterfall sensation in
your shower.

Take children to the seashore and make wishes on every seventh
wave. Make a wildlife pond. Even if you live hundreds of miles
from the ocean, its cleanliness and the preservation of its creatures,
such as whales, dolphins and seals, are burning issues, if we are to
have a heritage to pass on to future generations. Get involved in relevant conservation work, if you can, or make donations to
conservation organisations.

The Sky

The Sky is the realm of light and shadow, of Sun, Moon and stars.
If possible, visit a plain on a sunny day or at dawn and see the
hugeness of the Sun rising over the horizon; or stand in full
moonlight and absorb the magic through every pore.

Buy a sky map for your computer or a sky globe, and through
the year watch the wheeling of the stars and constellations, their
different rising and setting times, their appearance and disappear-
ance and the progress of the planets, the wanderers.

Study birds in their natural habitats and in conservation areas
and most importantly pass on this knowledge to the next generation, who may be able to identify imaginary space monsters but
not know the names of the birds in their garden.

Work for clean air and to reverse global warming; fight for the
rainforests, for if we destroy the lungs of the planet our descendants
will choke because of our carelessness.

The Three Realms in Ritual

The sacred grove is the meeting point of the three realms and in the
centre is the sacred unifying fire that can be represented by a small
fire in a brazier, a lantern containing a nightlight, or a candle set in
a small pot or cauldron or sand. If you are being really complex,
and combining the elements and the realms, you can in formal
ritual use a fire symbol in the south of the circle for the fourth
element. Two sources of fire guarantee a dynamic ritual.

Experiment with all the ideas listed below and find one that works for you.

- Draw a small circle in the earth with a stick around your fire, so you can stand in the place of the fire and make offerings. You can then represent the three realms as three concentric circles extending outwards from the fire circle, drawn in the earth or on the sand; if working in a confined space or indoors, you can also create miniature circles with clay or in a sand box. In a miniature layout a small nightlight in a container can represent the central fire.

- As you will be facing inwards towards the fire during the ritual, it is probably best to have the Earth as the outermost circle, the beginning of the journey. You then look over the Sea towards the Sky, and above or beyond at the Sun, the heart of fire. An alternative is to have Earth as the central circle, enclosed by Sea within and Sky without. Make your own choice.

- Draw an entrance like a processional route from the west, where you will enter, cutting through the three realms/circles as a straight pathway to the central Fire.

- In the outermost circle of the Earth place symbols of the Earth, such as a dish of small fruits, nuts and flowers.

- In the middle circle of the Sea, set a dish of seaweed, sea salt, water plants such as water lilies, and ceramic dolphins or fish.

- In the innermost circle of the Sky have a dish of feathers, seeds, small mirrors to reflect the light and tiny paper kites.

- Make sure that you have one item for each realm that will burn easily and quickly, and try to make the objects of personal significance.

- Begin in the realm of Earth and carry with you a small dish in which to collect your flammable offerings.

- Facing east at the entrance of the Earth realm, towards the centre and the fire, state what you regard to be precious about the Earth, and as you do so begin to walk clockwise around the circle.

- When you have completed the circuit pick up a flammable Earth symbol, place it in your offerings dish and move into the middle circle of the Sea.

- Continue to do this for the realms of the Sea and the Sky. If you allow words to flow as you tread the realms, you may be surprised at your own eloquence.

- When you have all three flammable offerings in the centre, make an offering to the guardian of the fire from the gifts of each realm in turn, asking for healing to the three realms and also for anyone who may be ill or troubled. The less you ask for yourself, the more you will receive under cosmic blessings. This ritual is a good one for sending healing to species and places, as well as to people and specific animals. You might choose an example for each realm.

- When the tributes are burned thank the guardian of the fire. As you walk back around each circle in turn, still clockwise or sunwise, thank each of the guardians of the three realms in turn.

- You can carry out this ritual with other people, allowing them to represent the different realms and perhaps having one to act as guardian of the fire, to receive the blessings and burn them, adding personal prayers and blessings.

The Triskele

The triskele is, according to archaeological evidence, a genuine Celtic artefact, a three-armed symbol radiating from a central point sometimes contained within a circle. The Druid Revivalists associated this symbol with the three Celtic realms of Earth, Sea and Sky. Since the symbol takes the form of a rounded spiral with three arms radiating from a central point, turning counterclockwise, this would seem a valid association psychically.

When I visited the Celtic and Roman sections of the British Museum in London, I found a number of examples of the triskele on artefacts that would suggest it was a ritual symbol for the Celts. For example, there was an iron linchpin with a cast bronze triskele in the centre dating from 300 to 200 BC. It was excavated in East Yorkshire and came from a chariot burial, the chariot probably being intended to carry the deceased to the Otherworld.

A cast bronze horn cap triskele dating from 200 to 100 BC was found in Saxthorpe in Norfolk. Its precise function was unknown. In formal Druidic ritual, a horn is sometimes blown in the centre of the circle to summon the Wise Ancestors and so you can make a speculative leap and link the triskele with this if you wish (as I do).

The triskele symbol is also a good psychic symbol to represent the continuing spiral of life in the Celtic world: birth, death and the afterlife, followed by rebirth. I have a permanent one made from stones in my garden that forms a source of power when I walk it.

Creating Your Triskele Amulet

Practise drawing your triskele (*see below*) until you can complete it in sweeping, anti-clockwise movements from the centre. Then draw a circle around it to enclose the protection.

The triskele is also sometimes represented as three interlinked spirals within the circle, recalling the Mother Goddess spirals on passage graves such as Newgrange near Dublin in Ireland.

- To create your amulet, which you can wear as a charm, you can use almost any natural substance. It may be a metal or wooden disc on which you can etch the triskele. Or you could paint one on a crystal, or draw one on thin paper or papyrus and roll it into a tiny gold or silver tube that you can wear around your neck. You can also make one in clay.

- My own favourite method is to melt a small beeswax candle on a metal tray and etch the symbol in the melted wax. When it is cool, you can keep it in white silk or a tiny purse.

• You can also draw your triskele in silver pen on black paper and use it for meditation.

• Create a large triskele within a circle, on a beach, on earth in woodland, or on a hard surface outdoors in chalk. Use it where you can – even in a town the interconnected realms will create a surge of Earth energy that is empowering as well as protective.

• It is also possible to create a talismanic or empowered triskele to bring the cumulative power as well as the protection of the triple realms into your life. You may need this because you have reached a change point in your life, or because you have an important venture – earthly or spiritual – to undertake.

• To empower your triskele, place it on a white cloth, then sprinkle it with a few dried rose petals or pot pourri. As you do so, say, 'Earth, Sky and Sea, bring power to me.' Next make a clockwise circle of water around the triskele, saying, 'Sea, Sky and Earth, bring truth to birth.' Finally, using a pine or fennel incense stick for the power of the Sky, make an equal-armed triangle in the air enclosing the amulet, saying 'Sky, Earth and Sea, by triple decree, by the power of Sky, from low to high, from Earth and Sea, blessings be.'

In the next chapter we will work with the power of the Sun as a source of energy and inspiration in the everyday world and the realms of magic.

4

Working with the Sun

If witchcraft is the religion of the Moon, modern Druidry is, it is often said, the religion of the Sun. Its public rituals are performed in the *eye of the Sun*, mainly during daylight, although some begin or end in the dark, for example on the solstices (*see pages 171–3*). Of course, that is not the whole story, for Druidry is above all other things the spirituality of balance. The Moon is, as I describe in the next chapter, also important for Druidesses. It enables them to get in touch with their own bodily and emotional cycles, and to work with the energies of the night as well as the day.

The Sun and Druidesses

In a number of cultures, including Classical Greek and Roman mythology, the Sun is regarded as a masculine force. However, from Celtic myths, recorded from early medieval times, come tales of Celtic Sun Mothers.

Sulis, Brighid, Grainne and Aine are Sun Goddesses within the modern Celtic tradition, and ceremonies dedicated to the Celtic Aine and Grainne survived until well into the twentieth century in Ireland, where they were conducted as folk rituals at the height of summer (*see pages 161 and 164*).

Exploring the Female Power of the Sun

The Sun is an empowering and life-bringing symbol for Druidesses today, and I have found that its power has special qualities at different times of the day and year. To discover these walk out in sunlight, especially sunshine that appears unexpectedly on a winter's day, allowing light to warm every pore; splash in puddles of sunlight after rain; or paddle or swim in the light in the sea or a swimming pool.

Observe sunlight rippling on water, colouring the leaves, casting a momentary brilliant disc of radiance in the midst of shadows. Go out at sunrise, noon and dusk, and experience the different energies that flow through nature, the urban streets and you.

In your journal record the images, words, emotions and impressions that the Sun evokes in you at different times of the day, the year (*see* Chapter 12 for seasonal change points) and in different places, noting how you feel intense heat, clear sunlight or a gentle evening glow. In the modern world it is now possible for us to move from summer to winter and back again in twenty-four hours. As we fly around the globe, we can watch the Sun set and within a few hours or so rise again. Technology too can offer us via computer or satellite images of the midnight Sun in the north, of the blazing orb rising huge over the horizon in a desert, of sunlight shimmering on snow, of eclipses, and of the Sun's rays shafting a stone circle, or a cathedral labyrinth, or suddenly illuminating the entrance of an ancient tomb on the Midsummer or Midwinter Solstice.

Making Sun Water

One way in which you and others can imbibe the healing and energising powers of the Sun is by using Sun water that you have made. This is most potent when it is made on the morning of the Longest Day, the Summer Solstice, around 21 June (21 December in the southern hemisphere), during a partial eclipse or, if you are lucky enough to have one in your region, a total eclipse of the Sun. However, you can also make Sun water on any day when the Sun is shining from dawn until noon.

- If you are in a gloomy weather period or live where the Sun shines only briefly during the winter, you can add extra-clear quartz crystals plus a citrine to your water to boost the solar energies.

- Fill a brass or gold-coloured bowl or one of clear crystal (like an old-fashioned fruit bowl) with pure spring water. You can use bottled still mineral water, much of which comes from former sacred springs. Otherwise use rainwater collected in a vessel placed on a low roof or from a water butt, unless you are in an area of high pollution.

- Add three clear crystal quartz stones and, if you wish, surround the bowl with flowers of sunshine yellow.

- Leave the water from dawn until noon, or until the Sun is directly overhead in your time zone (put the bowl out overnight if you do not wish to get up early, covered with fine mesh to keep out any pollution; you may get some additional lunar powers).

- Bottle the water in tiny, clear, yellow or gold-coloured glass bottles with stoppers. Antique and craft fairs are good sources of these. Keep some of these filled bottles in the fridge to drink.

- Add a few drops of your Sun water to baths, splash it on your brow and hairline if you feel stressed or spaced out, or sip it to give you an infusion of energy and confidence. You can also energise plants and animals with a few drops, or use it as sacred water in ritual.

Healing with Sun Water

Sun water will help to heal people, animals, places and species if you infuse the purpose and the name of the patient or threatened place when the water is almost ready.

Wait until the Sun is shining directly into your bowl just before noon. Stir the water three times clockwise with a clear crystal pendulum or pointed quartz crystal, naming the focus and the purpose of the water. You can either prepare small individual bowls or bottles, or infuse the water with a number of purposes, stirring separately for each; either method works.

- Ask for healing from the highest forces of light and, as you stir the water, name the person and the illness or sorrow, the place and the cause of pollution or despoliation, and infuse it with blessings.

- When you have stirred the water, look on to its surface and visu-alise the face of the person, the animal or the threatened place restored to beauty and whisper 'Blessings be,' before dedicating the water to the next subject.

- Pour out the prepared water into individual glass bottles. Add a tiny crystal of quartz to each; tie each bottle with a gold ribbon.

- If you know the person you wish to give healing to well and they are present, you can open the bottle in sunlight, supplementing this with golden candles or a fibre-optic lamp on a dark day, so that it shines golden, and anoint their brow with a few drops. You can create your own healing words, based on love and caring.

- With an animal, rub a little of the warmed water close to its heart. If the animal is in pain and does not want to be touched, add the water to the drinking bowl, and place the bowl in brilliant light.

- You can sprinkle the water around a photograph of absent people, animals, species or places, suffusing the picture in brilliant light, while expressing your concerns and desire for healing. If the place is local or you can visit it, sprinkle the water on the ground or in the polluted water source if that is what you wish to heal.

- Send the rest of the bottle of Sun water to the sick person to whom you wish to give healing, with a small citrine as a gift, saying that it comes with your love in a note also explaining how and why you made it.

Awen and the Sun

If you attend or watch a modern public Druidic ceremony, you will hear those assembled and may be asked to join in calling nine Awens. Rather like the Buddhist mantra *Aum*, this is the Druidic name for the life and inspirational force of generation behind the universe that is linked with the Sun. Some Druidesses identify this as the sound that called forth creation. Books will tell you that this is pronounced *AAH-oo-en*, or *AAH-oo Wen*, or as three equally weighted syllables in a monotone. But, in practice, when you have a lot of people calling Awen in the dusk or early dawn light, the sounds merge so that it becomes more like the sound of the sea, of wind rippling through fields of corn or the call of the birds going to roost at night, especially when the call is made on a rising note.

Practise calling Awens, three, six or nine times, in a monotone. Then, as though you were ascending or descending scales, sing in a cave, a tunnel, in dense woodland, in a valley of rocks or an old quarry, and let the echoes swell your voice. Sing it as you walk, dance it in your grove and swim it through water, so that the sound will become a part of you, like *Aum*, a creative sound that fills you with power and certainty, and you will no longer worry whether you are saying it correctly.

Awen is also a symbol drawn by Druidesses and Druids as a way of invoking and sending blessings (it is popular at the end of Druidic emails and can be downloaded from the Internet for non-commercial purposes). It consists of the three rays of the Sun.

I have seen two completely different explanations for its form. One says that at the time of the Midsummer sunrise, the Sun casts three spreading rays of light, the Awen, which open the gates of Annwyn, the doorway to the Otherworld. The other view is that they represent the points at which the Sun rises on the equinoxes and solstices, that is due east at the time of the equinoxes, as represented by the central bar of the Awen. At the time of the Summer and Winter Solstices the Sun rises in the east-north-east and the east-south-east respectively, so these directions would form the bars on either side.

While the concept of Awen and its solar connections are popularly regarded as Revivalist, rather than an ancient Celtic symbol, some Druidesses believe that Awen, translated as flowing spirit, may be an ancient concept that was Christianised. But the important fact is that it seems, both from my own work and other women's work, that it is a powerful solar psychic symbol.

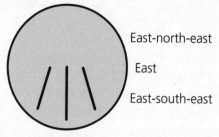

East-north-east

East

East-south-east

An Awen symbol showing the three rays of the Sun. On the right-hand side are shown the directions of the Winter and Summer Solstice sunrises.

The rays are sometimes positioned within the centre of a triple circle to represent the three Celtic realms, Earth, Sea and Sky, or the circles of existence and the passage of the soul (*see pages 199–200*, where you will find suggestions of books that describe this Revivalist and quite complex view of the universe), or simply enclosed in a circle.

Working with Awen

Now it is time to make and use this Sun symbol to access that doorway to the Otherworld and absorb the power of the Sun into our lives, winter or summer.

- Draw your Awen in sand or soil or create one out of seeds, nuts or twigs, and surround it with a circle to focus and concentrate its power. Alternatively, create one out of small stones or shells in your garden and surround it with an enclosing circle of pebbles (you could also use glass nuggets). Work in sunlight when you can, so that the circle will be filled with light and the pebbles or nuggets will gleam. In winter, if it snows, the Sun will melt away the whiteness, leaving the symbol intact. Indoors, you can create a miniature Awen from clay or on paper, or make one with tiny quartz and citrine crystals to catch the sunlight, using perspex rainbows and suncatchers at the windows, if necessary amplified by golden candles.

- Stand or sit facing south at the point where the three sunbeams converge. Work at the brightest part of the day, visualising brilliance if the day or season is dark.

- Visualise one of the beautiful Celtic Sun or Fire Goddesses haloed around the Sun (see the example of Brighid hanging her cloak on the Sun Wheel on page 47). Visualise the crone or Wise Woman Goddess Cerridwen directly ahead of you, stirring a cauldron of pure gold whose essence radiates as a rich rivulet of liquid gold around your circle. Feel also the golden soil of the Earth Mothers warming you beneath, heated by the molten volcanic forces, the Sun beneath the surface of the world.

- Breathe in the golden light through your nose, slowly and gently, exhaling darkness until you create a steady, continuous rhythm and are no longer aware of your breathing but only the inflow of light from all around you, above and beneath and around into every pore.

• As you continue breathing, visualise the light going upwards, from your toes right to the tips of your fingers, then downwards through the crown of your head, and inwards like a rushing waterfall of light, in which up is down, in is out and you are the light.

• Begin your call 'Awen', at first low and slowly, then higher and with greater intensity but maintaining a comfortable pitch so you do not tip over and lose the sense of control and stillness within the cascading light water.

• Continue until you can see light radiating from within you and you are connected with the source of power and inspiration.

• Hold the moment when you feel totally at one with solar power, then allow the Awens to slowly fade and become slower, until they are no more than a whisper and at last return to the heart of stillness and silence.

• Make a sign, perhaps the Awen, in the palm of your hand, knowing that if ever you are far from home or anxious you can recall your Sun circle and become once more connected to the light.

• If, as you work through this ritual, you place beside you or hold a clear quartz crystal or citrine within the circle it will become empowered. You can paint the Awen symbol on it in gold after the ritual to keep you powerful and protected.

• Allow the radiance also to fade slowly, knowing it is always with you though unseen, for you are a daughter of the light.

• Thank the Sun Goddess and wise Cerridwen who has watched over you while you worked. She may reward you with a few words of inspiration or a creative surge that can be manifest in your life

• If your Awen is only a temporary one, erase it. If it is permanent bury a small offering such as a crystal or a few herbs close to the sign.

Using the Inspiration of Awen

There are numerous ways of obtaining the inspiration of Awen. As you learn more about Druidry, you may find that your spiritual and psychic awareness spontaneously evolve. As your words become more measured and less impetuous and situation driven, so they will be wiser and, in times of quietness, may even assume a prophetic ring. This may seem frightening, but it is a natural development.

You may find creativity in all its forms permeating even seemingly mundane aspects of your life, filling them with beauty and meaning for yourself and those with whom you come into contact.

To the modern Druidess, especially one whose definition of inspiration may not be tinged with aspirations towards medieval bardship (and who is mercifully not inclined to keep people sitting on a freezing hillside listening to her poetic renditions), the flowing life force may assume more practical applications. The trend is spreading throughout Druidry, despite pockets of resistance, that it is a living faith, as much at home in the work place and the shopping precinct as in a grove or stone circle. It is seen as more important to practise than to preach.

Your Awen inspiration can prompt a period of channelled activity. This may involve problem solving and creative decision making, or channelling and developing healing powers to bring peace and reconciliation to colleagues, neighbours and even stressed strangers. You may paint rooms and houses as well as pictures to brighten the lives of others and yourself. Digging, planting and weeding gardens or window boxes, and nurturing new plant life, can be an act of Druidic faith, as can singing fretful children to sleep. Sculpting or putting up shelves, really caring about providing after-school centres for children, preserving areas of wildlife from developers by peaceful but determined effort – all help to spread positivity in a negative, cynical world.

An Awen Ritual – Opening the Doorway

There are times when inspiration is needed on the very deepest of levels, perhaps because an unexpected setback has shaken the roots of your confidence. We know the doorway is there in the Awen, and there may be times when we wish to look through it, although we may choose not to pass through it.

- Begin once more by creating your Awen within a circle. This time draw the three drops of inspiration falling into it. Draw them as dots above each of the three Sun rays. On the first (from the left) Awen ray put a dish of Sun herbs, such as bay, juniper, rosemary, sagebrush (broad-leafed sage), saffron and St John's wort.

- On the second Awen ray, set a golden candle, beeswax if possible, in a broad-based holder or on a small metal tray for safety.

- On the third Awen ray place a tiny, gold-coloured or clear glass dish of Sun water. If you work at about noon, the ideal time, you could have left your Sun water within the Awen circle to gather power from dawn; on each of the three drops of inspiration set a round crystal quartz.

- Sit within the circle in front of the Awen facing south with the three drops of inspiration furthest from you. Begin by carrying out the earlier ritual described above to fill yourself with radiance, but this time as you slow your Awens, maintain the vision of the radiance. Take a few grains of Sun herbs and drop them into the candle flame, saying 'Awen, ever-flowing stream, I bring Sun to your Sun. Grant me, I ask, one drop of your sacred inspiration to flow within me, brewed in the cauldron of the Mother.'

- Dipping the index finger of your power hand into the Sun water, drink a single drop and say 'Blessings be.'

- Repeat for the second and third drops, each time burning a few grains of herb and asking for inspiration, drinking the single drop and giving thanks.

- Following the third drop, after 'Blessings be,' add, 'Thus do I approach the doorway into light. I ask that I may see within what is right for me to know. I put my faith in the Sun.'

- Focus on the three crystals and allow them to merge with the Awen symbol, which will glisten pure gold and expand into a gold and crystalline doorway that will slowly open, revealing golden light.

- Blink and as you open your eyes you will see perhaps a single image framed against the radiance before it closes.

- Now, in turn, take each of the crystal drops and cast them into the Sun water. For each one, ask for creativity, inspiration or fertility in an area of your life that needs it. You may hear words in your head or see a sudden image in the water that will make sense in your dreams that night or during quiet reveries. Accept whatever you are given as a blessing.

- Sit quietly and when you are ready, blow out the candle, sending love and light to anyone you know who is sick or distressed.

- If your Awen is only temporary, as before, erase it. Before you do so, bury the three crystals and the remaining herbs near the centre. If it is a permanent garden Awen, pour the rest of the Sun water on it to purify it and again bury your offerings.

Over the months you may look for longer into the doorway, and you may wish to stand in the entrance. You need not be afraid that you will be carried off psychically into the Otherworld, and from the doorway you will see only light and beauty; in time you may have glimpses of your own unique vision of the Otherworld, what constitutes for each individual eternal happiness and peace.

The Celtic Druidesses lived much closer to nature than modern ones do. As high-ranking priestesses, they would also have probably been able to concentrate on Druidry, rather than having to care for the fields or worry about hauling the water from the river. Druidesses today usually have to combine their rituals and divinatory work with earning a living, and even in this liberated age doing most of the chores and caring for the family. We have no communities to support us or to allow us free access through our physical world without danger from other tribes.

So, until we begin our own special, final journey into eternity, we may have to be content with precious glimpses of magical realms, which fill us with the knowledge that our souls are immortal and that this is only the first part of a forgetful staging post of our voyage through many lifetimes into the lands of radiance.

The Seasons of the Sun

In Chapter 12, on the Druidic Wheel of the Year, I have described the seasonal celebrations at the solar change points, the equinoxes and solstices whose differing energies allow us to work with their particular qualities and absorb these strengths into our own life, as we carry out rites like our ancestors did for the necessary turning of the seasonal wheel.

But within each day too, the Sun wheel turns; we can work at these solar highs and lows to restore our connection with nature and absorb the strengths we need. This does not have to be done with formal ritual. If you light a candle, for example, to welcome the dusk, and sit enfolded by the fading light, you can focus on a point on the horizon and ride the gentle daily downturn of the wheel. Of course, you may be a shift worker or still have a mountain of paperwork to complete before home time. Or you may have to brace yourself for the arrival home of the family and all their different demands. But that brief oasis of stillness at dusk can switch off the more frantic centres in your brain and bring a harmony to your spirit that will enable you to finish serenely in half the time, when all around you are fretting and twitching in overdrive.

Sun Times

The time of dawn varies each day and can be found in a diary or the weather section of a newspaper. Unless you live on the line marking GMT, the Sun will not be exactly overhead at noon, so work with your own local noon time when the Sun is directly above you. Dusk also varies each evening. When you have a free weekend or a few days, live by the four markers: dawn, noon, dusk and midnight. Experience the different energies out of doors and following the rhythms of the sky as our ancestors did, before the advent of electricity. If you are afraid of the dark, work just before dawn initially so that you can witness the inevitable return of the light – to our ancient forebears this was a matter of trust, so if you can learn to trust again, you will relax.

Dawn

Dawn is a very special point in Druidry as the sunrise at the Midsummer or Midwinter Solstice especially symbolises the birth or rebirth of light. Many stone circles and passage graves are aligned to sunrise on special days; in the Christian tradition too, the importance of these special sunrises is recognised. For example, in the centre of the large, octagonal labyrinth in Amiens Cathedral in Picardy in France, a shaft of sunlight filters on the Midwinter and the Summer Solstice (around 21 June).

The centre of the labyrinth in the nave of Amiens Cathedral corresponds with the Spring Equinox and is represented in ritual by facing east. However, since the Sun only rises in the true east (and sets in the west) on the equinoxes, you may wish to work with the actual position of the Sun in the sky when dawn breaks.

It is worth rising early to sit or stand and witness the beautiful patterns as darkness retreats, sometimes not without struggle. You will see that dawns are different at various times and places – in winter, in summer, in bad weather or during a clear period, over plains, in deserts, over the sea, and above mountains and forests. Walk in the quiet of the city before it wakes, or in the countryside, or watch the darkness receding over the sea, leaving the scarlet-tinged waves. Every dawn is a Spring Equinox written small, a resurrection, and the birth of new hope.

Today is the day you anticipated or feared during many sleepless nights or anxious moments. So walk into the dawn with courage, yelling your defiance or your belief that you will win through or that this day will be absolutely the best one ever, because you will make it so.

Noon

'Be not Sad, be as the sun at midday' says a passage in the I Ching. Whether the Sun is beating down or hiding behind sullen clouds, the noon energies are powerful and so are you. Therefore at every noon, as at every Summer Solstice, count your blessings. If they are thin on the ground, seize some of that Sun power, reflecting it through a crystal quartz sphere (even the tiniest one will be bursting with Sun power). Allow the reflected light to fill you with energy and assurance that all will be well.

Remember, too, to channel the light and power of noon into your healing work, holding your crystal quartz or crystal sphere (size does not matter) to reflect the light. Speak into the crystal words of healing, and direct the rays or light beams to whoever or whatever needs healing, person, animal or place. You may be rewarded by a sudden, tiny rainbow in the centre of the crystal, confirming that positive thoughts return to the sender threefold.

Dusk

'Never let the Sun go down on anger,' my late mother used to say. This is the daily message of dusk, writ large in the Autumn Equinox. Whatever has been gained or lost merges into the darkness; with it we can drain resentment and regrets.

If you are near water, dusk is a good time to cast a stone or a flower expressing regrets. In the earth, bury the stone of a fruit or a few seeds that will in the future bear fruit and blossom from what has been perhaps too dearly learned. As you light your dusk candle if you are at home (easier after long summer nights when dusk is late), you can speak words of blessings on your enemies and consign the day to be reworked in the darkness.

Then, as shadows soften harsh emotions, you can if you need to send reconciliatory letters or emails, make soothing phone calls, or speak in person your love or forgiveness, if only to yourself if another person is implacable.

If all is well in your world, you can share your own peace and happiness, perhaps with someone who always goes home alone and wishes it were otherwise; with a friend or family member far from home in a hotel room or at college, who draws the curtains on the darkness, or with a neighbour who would welcome a brief visit before you settle down either contentedly in your own castle or with loved ones for the evening.

As I said earlier, you can make a dusk oasis even if you are at work, and then perhaps light a candle and have a simple dusk ritual later when you do arrive home, reading a list of the names of people and places you know are in need.

Midnight

Midnight may appear to be an unlikely Sun time, but it is an important one as it corresponds with the Midwinter Solstice rebirth of light. Just as sunset began a new day for the Celts, so in the modern world midnight is the transition.

You may be awake at this time because you have been out socially or entertaining friends, or you may be a shift worker or have returned home late from work or travelling. Or you could be lying awake worried about people, or tomorrow, or next year, and this is a time when dragons can loom large.

We all know the saying 'the darkest hour is before the dawn' and it has a ring of truth. But in another time zone the Sun is shining brightly and we know, unlike our distant forebears, that the Sun does not disappear into the sea or back into the womb of the Earth Mother to sleep until morning.

Midnight too is the time of the Wise Ancestors. They are not frightening phantoms who will haunt you, but gentle essences stretching back through time, who spiritually and genetically have made you what you are. Also with you at the midnight hour are the guardians of the night, who protect you in these waking hours before dawn, and who will carry you into peaceful sleep if you lie down and let their faces form.

But first allow to float away on the dark tide that even now is turning, all those things from the past, the old voices of doubt or unfair criticism that wounded us when we were children and vulnerable and may return to haunt us in the night. Let float also what cannot now be; name your worries and whatever keeps you awake or whatever surfaces when you are trying to relax. Burn all this in a dark blue candle as black threads or strands of wool. When you are done, send the light as you extinguish it to the Sun, knowing that it will return to light the dawn.

In the next chapter we will work with the alter ego of the Sun, the Moon, and its gentler but equally magical energies.

5

Working with the Moon

The Moon is the alter ego of the Sun. Since the Celtic new day, it is told in Celtic myth and folklore, began at dusk, at the major festivals moonlight was important both for providing light and ritually, because it signified the presence and blessings of the Moon Mother. A Full Moon on a festival, rising around dusk, is in magical ritual regarded as especially mystical and fortunate. The extreme Midwinter Full Moonrise, which occurs every eighteen years and seven months, once marked a complete ritual cycle, and on this day the rebirth of light was especially potent because it was mingled with the tides of change signified by the Full Moon.

The Significance of the Lunar Calendar

The Moon was, before the time of formal calendars, probably the marker used for noting regular occurrences throughout the year. Some events, such as the migration or return of certain birds, or the arrival of the herds, occurred regularly after a set number of Moons. For a woman the Moon has links with her bodily calendar. Women menstruated each month, traditionally at the time of the Old Moon, and seemed to be most fertile when the Moon was full. A pregnancy lasts ten lunar months.

Since the Moon appeared to grow, become full, then decline and finally disappear, only to return two and a half days later, the Moon was credited with the powers of fertility for animals, people and, later, crops. At some period, the Moon became mythically linked with three aspects of womanhood identified in the Triple Goddess, Maiden, Mother and Crone, who in Celtic myths were called three sisters.

The popular names given to the cycle of Full Moons described the powers and privations of each month. These folk calendars accorded well with the agricultural year, and some farmers and gardeners still plant on the three days before the Full Moon for maximum growth, a botanically proven phenomenon.

Specific Moons also heralded times when the roads were sufficiently dry for travelling to markets, fairs or to seek justice, so that people could make plans to travel two or three Moons ahead. Before the spread of the written word, these traditions were handed on orally, enshrined in myths that reminded listeners of the stages of the seasonal and agricultural year. Even today, in parts of Spain and Italy, crops are harvested or pruned on particular saints' days as reminders of these early *aides-mémoire*.

The lunar calendar is therefore embedded deep within all of us through our distant ancestors. Spiritually it thus may seem more meaningful than the solar calendar that was imposed by patriarchal Sky God worshippers, such as the Romans.

Darkness and Light

We are not certain how the present knowledge of the times and seasons that are used as the focus of modern witchcraft and Druidic practices came into being. Certainly, by early medieval times come complaints by clerics of peasantry still following festivals linked to the agricultural year with the focus on non-Christian goddesses or gods. But in both modern magic and Druidry, light is not superior to darkness and darkness is not regarded as evil, but as preceding light and representing the nurturing womb of the Earth Mother.

The Celtic myths indicate that the dark half of the year began at the Celtic New Year on 1 November and the light half followed at the beginning of summer on 1 May. It would seem that the new day began in darkness at dusk. Whether this is historically factual or not, during the winter before the advent of widely available artificial lighting, ordinary people certainly spent part of their waking time in darkness before going to bed. In this way the Moon assumed an important role in their lives.

The Celtic Lunar Calendar

The Roman historian Pliny reported that the Druids calculated their months and years by lunar time. Although we also have some archaeological knowledge of the Celtic lunar calendar to support this, nevertheless a great deal of inspiration has filled in the gaps created by time and has either clarified or muddied the waters, according to your perspective.

The archaeological source of our knowledge of Celtic lunar calculations is the Coligny calendar. This survives in fragments of a huge bronze plate measuring, when it was intact, 1.5 metres by 1 metre. The calendar, named after the location where it was discovered in eastern France in 1897, was engraved in Gaulish, but with Roman letters and numbers. Because it contains Roman letters, it has been approximately dated to around the beginning of the first millenium BC at the earliest, although the information on it may be older. Julius Caesar refers to it.

The calendar has twelve cyclical Moon months, and it seems from the sixty-two consecutive months recorded that an additional two months were included (one every two-and-a-half to three years, consisting of thirty days each). The Coligny Calendar ran from Full Moon to Full Moon. Similar calculations are etched on the stones of Knowth, near Newgrange in Ireland, one of the most sacred megalithic sites in that country.

Another theory favours following the Coligny calendar, but suggests that the Romanised Gauls replaced in its creation an earlier Celtic calendar that was thirteen lunar months long, based on the actual Full Moons in the sky before the year completely revolved.

Working with the Moon Months

If you have access to the Internet, there are many excellent on-line lunar calendars/calculators for the Coligny system. Some lunar almanacs also include the Coligny and tree months.

Even if you have access to these sources, there is no substitute for looking in the sky and matching Moon to name. Most importantly, go back to the practices of the people who made their notches and related the Moon in the sky to what was happening in the natural world and to the crops or herds.

Use and adapt the calendar to your daily and ritual life. If you live mainly in town, you can follow the monthly lunar energies by watching the changing leaves in city squares and escaping to the countryside and coast at weekends. But you may also want to adapt the Moon names to the world in which you live. So if planting seeds has less relevance than filling in the annual tax returns at the end of January, you may want to change the name of the Full Moon that shines as you struggle with your paperwork, or a least find a month with a name like Claim-time or Arbitration to fit it and rearrange the Moons accordingly. If you live in the southern hemisphere or a hot climate with different seasons, you will need to begin your Moon calendar in a different place, maybe six months on, for your summer's end will not be with the September Moon. Equally, in the northern parts of Scandinavia and north-eastern Europe, your summer and your returning birds will come much later.

It is not the calculations and the set names that are important; it is writing your personal lunar calendar, living by it and celebrating the coming of the Full Moons ritually. If your Moon times are out of step with the solar clock, have a double-date system in your diary so that you still keep business arrangements and appointments, and remember birthdays by the modern date, but know that these occasions also occur on the third day of the Migrating Geese or whatever you call the Moon in the sky.

If you want consistency, use the thirty days of your magical thirteenth month, called Caillos, *no time* in the Coligny calendar, when there is a period of unseasonable weather or great natural upheavals, since it is associated with transitions either in nature or in lifestyle. Keep this spare month for every two-and-a-half to three years to catch up, or use it when a Moon name does not feel right for what is going on – otherwise roll with the Moons in the sky.

Because of the irregular orbit of the Moon and the tilt of the Earth, lunar months vary slightly in length and occasionally you get two Full Moons in a solar month (the second referred to as a blue Moon); some months are naturally shorter than others, but then so are solar ones.

The following chart shows Celtic names for the lunar months I have collected from a variety of sources and adapted to my personal life as a Druidess, living as close to nature as I can while earning a living using technology. I have suggested areas for ritual for each month, and after the chart you will find a sample Full Moon ritual.

Coligny name	Full Moon date	Ritual
Samnios: seed fall	October/November	Making an end to what is not fruitful; drawing up realistic plans for the coming year.
Dumannios: the coming of deep darkness	November/December	Bringing light into the darkness; seeking inner as well as outer illumination and inspiration.
Riuros: the time of the long coldness	December/January	Material security, the home and family.
Angantios: staying at home	January/February	Acceptance of life as it is; seeking joy in what we have, and not fretting for what we have not.
Ogronios: the time of shining ice	February/March	The stirring of new hope and trust; releasing slowly the potential that has been frozen in the winter.
Cutios: the time of the winds	March/April	Change; clearing away stagnation and inertia.
Glamonios: growing green shoots	April/May	New horizons and opportunities; fertility.
Simiuisonnos: bright time or the time of dancing	May/June	Joy; permanent relationships; maximising opportunities.

Coligny name	Full Moon date	Ritual
Equos: the time of the horse	June/July	Travel; moves of all kinds; domestic or career expansion.
Elembiuos: claim time	July/August	Justice; promotion; recognition and financial gain.
Edrinios: the time of arbitration	August/September	Reaping what has been sown; abundance; assessing life and resources with a view to shedding what cannot be used.
Cantios: song Moon	September/October	Final burst of energy for tasks undone; salvaging relationships and missed opportunities.

Each month, as near to the night of the Full Moon as you are able, try to carry out a ritual to welcome its energies into your life (they extend a day or two on either side of the Full Moon). You can work alone, with family and friends, or with a group. Even if you really are busy, try to spend a few minutes in the full moonlight breathing in the silver light through your nose very slowly, and exhaling any darkness or negativity as a sigh. Whether informally or as a ritual, it may help to focus on one of the Celtic Moon Goddesses.

I have already mentioned Arianrhod, the beautiful and mystical Goddess of Reincarnation and the Full Moon who controlled the silver wheel of the stars and took the souls of slain heroes and heroines to be restored. You can also work with Cerridwen, the Welsh Lunar Goddess (*see page 163*), Ethiniu, Goddess of the North Star (*page 92*), Ana, the Mother Goddess (*page 161*), Arduinna, Gallic Mistress of the Forest (*page 161*), Blodeuwedd, Goddess of Flowers (*page 162*), and Rhiannon, Lady of the Otherworld and Dreams (*page 166*). You can, if you prefer, work with the Moon as Mother.

A Full Moon Ritual

For my Full Moon ritual I will use the example of Cantios, the Song Moon, and the September/October Full Moon. This is my own favourite, as I try to pack everything possible into the remaining days and evenings before my beloved caravan closes for the winter. While I am working indoors in the van, I may be huddled over the fire, but outdoors I squeeze out every last drop of autumn sunshine and wrap up against the chill if it is not raining so that I can sit outside and watch the stars.

Nature is aware of the imminent move, too. The telephone wires are thick with small birds, eager to be away to the warmer climates and no longer so interested in lingering to eat seeds. The geese from the nearby wildlife sanctuary are practising for their long flight to Canada, and although all is singing and cheerful there is a bittersweet feeling in my heart of being left behind.

Although this ritual is Cantios centred, it can easily be adapted to any other Moon, using almost identical tools and incenses. You can either use the silver bells as I suggest, or tie a branch with symbols of the different Moons: feathers, seasonal fruits, tiny corn sheaves or knots for the harvest Moon, coloured ribbons for May time or mistletoe towards the Midwinter Solstice Moon (*see also page 75*).

You can decorate the staff you generally use (*see pages 15–16*), or keep one of willow or alder wood, both Moon trees, or the traditional apple or fruit-bearing bough, for your lunar rituals.

Modern Druidess ceremonial wands are sometimes made from apple boughs, still with apples on them, as a symbol of an autumn Moon, and hung with silver bells or tiny silver balls, the colour and metal of the Moon. You can raid your Christmas decorations for the latter; they can be used for any Moon. Before the Full Moon rises, spend time decorating your staff. If you are working with others, you can decorate your grove with symbols of the Moon, for example silver ribbons and white flowers, as well as with symbols of your specific Moon – even discarded tax calculations can be cut into streamers, sprayed silver and attached to branches or plants.

Here is how to proceed.

- On the evening of the Full Moon, as it first appears, light a large silver candle in a sheltered place out of doors. Don't worry if the location is not beautiful. The smallest backyard or the tiniest balcony of a flat can bring you as close to the sky as standing on a moonlit shore.

- Set in front of the candle a silver bowl containing pure mineral water; the Moon should shine on the water, turning it silver, but the wax should not drip into it. Add three small moonstones to the water. In this way you can create Moon water.

- Place in a horseshoe behind the candle three sticks of jasmine or mimosa incense, to represent the Maiden, Mother and Crone aspects of the Moon.

- Finish decorating your Moon branch/staff, touching each symbol in turn (as many or as few as you wish), and asking for each a blessing for the month on yourself and all the creatures whose energies contribute to the overall quality of the month. My Cantios branch had tiny crab apples, fronds of herbs for rabbits, acorns for squirrels, feathers for migrating birds and nine silver bells.

- Ring each of the nine silver bells and let each sound pass into silence before creating the next. If you are working in a group, each of you can make a staff and ring the individual bells at the same time, having named your blessings separately.

- Using a taper, light each of the incense sticks separately from the candle, saying, 'First the Maiden, now the Mother, soon the Crone.' Hold the taper so it will flare in the candle, saying, 'But always light returns.'

- Standing in a circle, or if you are alone, facing the direction in which the Full Moon is rising, breathe in the silver light slowly and rhythmically and exhale darkness and doubt. If you are in a group, do not worry about synchronising breaths, for as you absorb the power, so will the collective harmonies mesh.

- If you are alone, you may sense your guardian is working with you. If you wish, as you become more experienced, the essence of wise Druidesses and Druids from ages past will join you if you ask them to at the beginning of the ritual.

- When you are filled with light, you will feel a stillness fall; now you can state slowly and quietly the powers you seek in your life/lives that relate to the special Moon power. In Cantios, I seek energy to keep up with the many tasks I have before me, but most important for me is to enjoy the last moments of light and warmth and not worry about tomorrow or next season and what will happen if I cannot return. Then turn to global issues and quite spontaneously ask for the lunar energies to aid problems in the wider world. Cantios energies are good for getting food and medical aid moving, for encouraging leaders to make a final push for peace even if a situation has reached an impasse, and for healing religious schisms.

- Now focus on the healing Moon water that has been created during the ritual and endow it with special blessings for any individuals or animals you know the water could help. For example, Cantios Full Moon water is especially good for relieving depression, anxiety or exhaustion.

- When you are finished, silently thank the Moon Mother and exhale three breaths of silver through your mouth as a sigh, thus sending the power of the ritual to those people, animals or places you have thought about or spoken of.

- Close the ceremony by ringing your bells nine more times, when each has faded adding 'Blessings be.'

- Leave the candle and the incense to burn through in a safe place and carry the Moon branch with you to place at your bedside to empower and protect you throughout the week. You can touch the symbols each night before you sleep and remind yourself of the qualities that grow within you.

- Leave the Moon water until dawn, covered with a mesh to prevent pollution, and use it in future rituals, to make drinks for friends, relations and work colleagues, to put into baths, and to water plants in the house or at work – you will find that over the months the gentle emotional healing of Moon water makes people more cooperative and less confrontational. Spare a few extra drops for a plant you see that is neglected or maybe abused (for example, used for cigarette butts in a reception area) and in time people will begin to respect it.

Other Moon Rites

You can celebrate other parts of the Moon cycle, not necessarily every month, but when you have the time or feel the need. These for me form essentially private rituals, that are, I believe, important especially for Druidesses who may, like most women, frequently become overwhelmed by personal, work and family commitments, and who may occasionally feel guilty about taking regular time out for spiritual work.

The Mistletoe Rite

One of the most fascinating lunar associations is with the mistletoe, the Druidic all-healer. Pliny describes a rite involving the rare mistletoe that grew on oak, the most sacred of the Druid trees. The ritual took place during what Pliny described as the sixth Moon. According to the Roman Julian calendar that began at the end of December, this Moon occurred around the Midsummer Solstice. Certainly, there is a precedent for Midsummer mistletoe rites throughout Europe, and later America.

This time can also be interpreted as the sixth day of the Moon, that is the sixth day after the New Moon, and because Pliny's report was secondhand, it is hard to be sure what he meant. The oak mistletoe, Pliny records, was harvested with a golden sickle by a Druid priest in a white robe (iron was not and still is not used for harvesting herbs by some practitioners of magic) and then caught in a white cloth or cloak – as an airborne plant, it could not be sullied by the earth. The literal translation of Pliny says that the mistletoe was caught in the cloth 'by others'.

Later versions of the Pliny myth and Victorian Romantic paintings suggest that these 'others' were virgins. Since mistletoe is associated with potency and fertility – according to Pliny it was given to barren animals after it was harvested – these cloak holders may have been virgin Druidesses, the lunar balance to the Sun King on the day of his greatest triumph, the Summer Solstice. The cutting was followed by the ritual sacrifice of two white bulls.

Working on the Sixth Day of the Moon

The Keltria Order of Druids celebrate their mistletoe rite on the sixth day of each New Moon (*see page 204*), and they focus on healing and balancing energies in their ceremonies as the Moon gently waxes.

Private Druidic rites of healing are also potent on this day. For although mistletoe berries are poisonous and you have to be an experienced herbalist to use the other parts medically, in modern medicine the healing properties of mistletoe are very impressive. Their uses include shrinking tumours, relieving heart conditions and leukaemia, reducing blood pressure and internal bleeding, boosting the immune system and increasing fertility.

Because the lunar energies are relatively stable during the first quarter of the lunar cycle, unlike during the more powerful but less stable Full Moon when it is in opposition to the Sun, a mistletoe ritual on the sixth day of the New Moon can create a quiet oasis in your life, when you can increase your personal harmony and sacred time for routine but valuable healing work.

You can find mistletoe growing in many parts of the world on a variety of trees and it will assume their specific magical qualities – for example, the cleansing and illuminating power of a pine tree. You could deliberately introduce mistletoe to grow on an oak tree – but be careful if you have children. Talk to your local garden centre or botanical garden, or buy spores by mail order. If you cannot obtain real mistletoe, you can buy silk fronds that you can use over and over again, and will only cut once and thereafter symbolically. This wonderful plant with its two-year cycle may offer flower buds in May that will blossom in February and you may in an older plant have all its stages of leaves, flowers and berries acting in harmony during its life cycle.

Your Mistletoe Rite

This rite can be as simple as you wish; you may decide to create a permanent, quiet healing place, a room or special table covered with a seasonal cloth where you keep crystals, candles and special treasures from the natural world that you are not currently carrying in your crane bag. If you can create a small sanctuary, the equivalent of a Druidess hut in the forest, it will increase in gentle power and loving energies as you work there.

Here's how to go about your mistletoe rite.

- On the night of the New Moon (you will not see the Moon in the sky for another two-and-a-half days at least), in the week before you begin your rite, create a mistletoe healing book. This can be a small, loose-leaf notebook whose cover you can decorate with images of the plant. In it write the names of anyone you know who is sick or needs harmony. Use a separate page for each person.

- Set your book where it will not be disturbed on a white silk square, and either circle it with sprigs of mistletoe or use pots of healing herbs (*see pages 122–37*).

- On the sixth night of the Moon, light a pure white or beeswax candle behind your healing book and replace any dry sprigs of mistletoe with fresh sprigs. If you are using silk mistletoe, burn mistletoe incense next to your candle. If you miss the actual night, work as close as you can to the sixth night. You may choose to work alone or with a trusted friend or family member with whom you are in harmony.

- Try to work where you can see the gently waxing or increasing Moon, or if it is cloudy set silver candles around the room and visualise its growing crescent.

- Open the book and start to read the names slowly one at a time, with any comments you have made about the nature of the illnesses or problems.

- Using a small silver or gold-coloured paper knife, cut a very tiny sprig of mistletoe for each name and place it in the page, saying each time, 'Blessings be; healing of the Moon, I ask and send in love and in humility.'

- When you have read all the names, close the book containing the mistletoe and allow the candle to burn through.

- The next morning, remove the mistletoe from the book and bury it. Keep your book updated during the month, adding new names and taking out the pages containing names of people who have recovered or moved beyond your personal sphere of influence.

New Moon Rites

The night of the New Moon is the exact opposite of the Full Moon – at this time the Moon vanishes from the skies. For this reason it is sometimes referred to as the Dark of the Moon. (Other cultures take the night of the New Moon as the time when the very first sliver of the waxing Moon is visible in the sky.)

When we can no longer see the Moon, we have to trust that it is still protectively circling our planet and will reappear again. This transition point is good for psychic housekeeping, so burn vervain, a herb associated with the New Moon in herbal folklore, in a purple candle. With the first leaf or grain you burn, name what you are casting off in the new month. As you burn the second, state what you hope to achieve spiritually and in any other aspect of your life that will be significant in the coming month.

Alternatively, light a slender, silver Moon candle and, instead of burning the vervain, float your leaves or grains of vervain in a bowl of water, again stating your intentions. You can tip this water away in the earth when you are finished.

In modern Druidess rituals a teaspoon of honey is offered to the Earth Mother by being placed in the soil (or a plant pot) in thanks. You might also like to dissolve a second spoon of honey in a mug of hot water for the Moon maiden and drink it, so absorbing what it is you wish to carry forward to the Crescent Moon. The Keltria Druids carry out their magical vervain ritual during the third quarter of the month.

Working with the Phases of Moon

Plot the course of the Moon for a month, relating what your diary or ephemeris says should be happening (allowing for time zone differences) to what you can see. (An ephemeris is a book listing the postions of the planets at particular times and dates, and also the movements and phases of the Moon throughout the year.)

It only takes a minute to focus on where the Moon should be and to allow yourself to merge with its essence. Although there are eight astronomical phases of the Moon, for the purposes of psychic work, if the Moon is increasing in size it is waxing until the point of the Full Moon, and the light increases from right to left. Then follows the day of the Full Moon and from that point, the energies are waning and the light decreases from right to left until you are back where you started.

Over the subsequent months, make more detailed notes. Sometimes these may be sketchy or non-existent because you are living in a demanding world and not in a forest hut with followers to bring you food and drink.

Children will help you and male partners especially enjoy fiddling with sky globes and talking knowledgeably about angles of ascent and descent. Try to find a fixed point in all four directions – a tree, a rooftop, a chimney pot – and see how the Moon varies as to where it is each night and each month on the same day; in time you will find that a pattern emerges.

Then start to anticipate your Moon moods. Women may find that their menstruation comes into line with the Moon phases, with peak fertility and ovulation occurring on the Full Moon. This works wonders for premenstrual syndrome. It is inexplicable but it may be that once you psychically align your body with the rhythm of the Moon over a period of time your physical cycles also move into line. A number of women who practise Moon magic, not just Druidesses, have confirmed this to me. But everyone can learn to harmonise with the differing energies, and for children hyper-activity can be lessened if, when the Moon is on the wane, the child is moved towards quieter activities and kept away from jarring noises.

The Waxing Moon

The time of the Crescent or Waxing Moon is a time of growth; this is why the old ritual of turning your money over on the Crescent Moon to make it grow is common to many cultures. Now is the time to consolidate those tentative plans from the vervain ritual. You will feel a gentle increase in energy and enthusiasm and can flow with this in initiating new plans or moving along existing ones. The more the Moon increases in size, the more powerful its energies – and your growing desire for action in every aspect of your life.

The Full Moon

You won't be taken by surprise when, at the time of the Full Moon, you are suddenly impatient for results, willing to put in extra effort and hours into any aspect of your life. But at the same time you may be experiencing that sudden yearning for change that has enabled the human race to evolve, if not always wisely. Look in the sky. The Moon is almost full and astrologically opposing the Sun. From the day or so before Full Moon until a day or so afterwards, you should channel your energies and not give way to unreasonable anger or impatience with others who are not as tuned in. Send off your novel, propose to the guy or girl of your dreams, ask your boss for more money, or say goodbye to someone or something that is holding you back. Use the surge of power to carry you to the crest of the wave.

The Waning Moon

Now the Moon is beginning to diminish. So it's back to the hut or garden shed appropriated during your Full Moon assertiveness, to sleep or mutter incantations as you create exotic brews. At least, that is the theory, because of course we still have to work and take care of the home while the Moon wanes in potency. Family members, friends, colleagues and the ticket collector on the train may be extra cranky as they try to vent their free-floating irritability and desire to be left alone. Children in contrast respond to waning lunar energies by running around faster and faster, tripping over and breaking things, and then complaining bitterly that it was not their fault.

You, of course, as a wise Druidess are gently applying the brakes to those in free fall around you, putting off non-essential decisions and confrontations that will be forgotten by the next waxing phase. If you can fit in an extra catnap or miss a scheduled leisure activity to sit by candlelight or walk slowly in the woods, you will be paced and not too exhausted to start anew.

Now is the time to consign all the bad, sad things of the month into the cosmos or the Earth, to be restored and reformed into positivity. You can bury seeds, or cast feathers on the wind, or stones or flowers into water.

This is in many ways the most psychic of all the phases. For, as you move away, whenever you can, from earthly activity and the frantic schedules that can rule leisure as well as work time, you may find that your dreams become richer, your inner imaging processes more vivid and your divination work more spontaneous, as conscious energies slow down and your innate powers guide you.

In the next chapter we will use these intuitive energies to look into the future and to the unseen realms for guidance on our life path.

6

Oracles and Divination

Interpretation of the symbols present in the natural world and their ability to guide human action is, to me, the core of Druidic work, the kernel within the nut, the seed within the fruit. It is something that unfolds over the months and years, always revealing new depths, however far along you are already on your spiritual path.

For the oracles of Druidry are primarily those of the voices of the natural world, the Wise Ancestors (*see* Chapter 10) and, above all, our own inner wisdom that can find tongue in the running waters or the wind.

Interpreting the Wisdom of Nature

As you work in the forest you will begin to hear and understand the voices in the leaves. You may see images as sunlight ripples a pool or a flock of birds wheels overhead. What you need to do to create a personal integrated oracular system is to collect, sort and analyse the myriad multi-layered symbols you encounter in dreams and divination. These are the keys that in time will unlock the inter-connected pathways between past, present and future.

Some basic interpretations of these symbols can be found in the different chapters as you read this book, for example the significance of different trees (*see* Chapter 7), and of animals and birds (*see* Chapter 9). But even these are only templates, and you may decide to create your own interpretations and variations in meaning according to the context in which the symbols appear. This will enable you to develop a unique and very valuable symbol system you may wish to hand on to others.

The greater your direct experience of nature, the richer your symbol system will become. Embrace each sensation and walk in wild conditions as well as on sunny days; a keen wind whipping up litter in a desolate urban corner has much to teach of the need to allow the winds of change to blow through life and clear the debris, painful though this may be.

Details are important, too, whether in waking visions, dreams or divination. As well as the focal image or images, there may be six or seven background features to the experience. If taken into account, these may modify or even change your initial interpretation of a situation concentrating only on the core symbol. Also in dreams and divination, natural symbols can provide the time frame according to whether rain clouds are coming towards you, moving away or delivering a refreshing shower to an existing drought-ridden area.

Creating Your Own Symbol System

Each time you receive a vivid image or are struck by the significance of some natural phenomenon, write it down in your journal. If, as I suggested, you are using a temporary working folder and then copying your insights into a more permanent record, you may find it helpful to have a set of rough alphabetical pages for symbols, or to use a sorting programme on your computer as I did to bring order to my chaotic scribbling. Even if an image does not immediately evoke feelings or impressions, note it down anyway. When you have time, sit quietly by candlelight in your grove or your healing place and repeat the name of the image softly over and over as a mantra until impressions come.

In dreams, you may find that a particular island or house constantly recurs, although you may not recognise it. Analyse the feelings it invokes in you: these may be joy, peace and a sense of loss when the dream ends. This recurring place may be an ancient ancestral home, a significant dwelling in a past life, or it may be a recollection of past times unrelated to you personally, cast up by the cosmic memory bank either because you need to find the place, or to act on the feelings it invokes, to improve your present life path.

Acting as a Wise Counsellor

Druidic oracles have little to do with fortune telling and, like all good devices for deciding a person's future path, may replace a seemingly open-and-shut issue with other, more pertinent questions that the seeker must answer him or herself.

The more interactive divination is, the more potent it becomes. If you are scrying (seeking images in water) for another person, ask them what images they perceive, for example in a bowl of water lit by candlelight. If an image or words come spontaneously into your mind when casting an oracle for a friend, ask for input on the meaning of the symbol in their life. The other person will usually reveal that it has deep personal significance and give some vital information that helps you to build on the symbol. Above all, the two greatest gifts you can offer are time and acceptance of the validity of the other person's point of view, even as you try to suggest ways out of what may seem a self-imposed spiral of difficulty.

Learning from the Celtic Seers

We know something about Druidic seers from Celtic myths and poetry (*see page 139* for details of the Bard Taliesin). And do you remember the Gallic innkeeper Druidess who prophesied the bright future of Diocletian?

Druidesses, it seemed, even advised the deities, although the myths obscure the god/hero/king boundaries. Another anonymous Druidess told Balor, the old Sun and Fire God, that his grandson would bring about his downfall. To prevent this, Balor locked up his virgin daughter Ethiniu in a glass tower in the sky. However, the hero Cian was drawn to find her and from their only meeting Lugh, the young God of Light was conceived and eventually overthrew his grandfather.

Using Prophecies Wisely

It may seem very simplistic, given the fierceness of clan battles, to suggest that Balor, once he had heard the prophecy, might have done better to have encouraged his daughter to marry and bear children with an approved heir. His grandson might have then been on the same side in battle and the succession would have passed naturally in the due time without bloodshed (or at least without his grandson wielding the executioner's spear). This leaves a real dilemma for would-be prophetesses and prophets. If you see something bad, should you reveal it? Substitute yourself for the Druidess and consider how you would react to an all-too familiar modern dilemma. Balor or Mrs Balor comes to ask you if their current marriage is going to end in divorce. The alarm bells ring.

Divination may confirm that the marriage is in serious trouble. So divorce is a fairly cut-and-dried prediction. But then your wise guardian digs you in the ribs, reminding you that the current path might change quite dramatically by what is probably more or less random fortune – unless you drop the stone of doom.

The root situation might change through an unexpected sudden input of money that eases underlying strains; a job offer may bring a new location and new start; a health scare might focus priorities; an unplanned pregnancy after a temporary reconciliation, or one too many bottles of wine, may change the entire board game. All these and many other scenarios may cause a shift in perspective.

Then, of course, there are deliberate decisions made by the parties concerned – one or both might decide to try to rekindle love, or a third party muddying the waters may get cold feet when they meet the truculent adolescents who come as part of the deal; the straying partner might find that the rubbish has to be put out even in a love nest.

The easy part is uncovering and interpreting the images and offering the quick fix. But Druidesses must be altogether more measured in their responses. This is where you twist yourself into psychic knots and peer through those mists of time, listening to faint echoes until your inner ear aches, in order to produce a series of viable and creative options to be explored on the earthly plane before the matter can be resolved.

Whether you sit under a waterfall wrapped in a bull hide, watch the clouds, lie in total darkness and stillness waiting for inspiration, interpret the flight of birds, look into the flames or water, or cast tree staves (*see* Chapter 7), divination is all about the real lives of flesh-and-blood people. The more our oracular abilities unfold, the more we become aware of what a very heavy responsibility we are assuming when we seek to walk in the shoes of others for even a few steps.

The Tools of Natural Divination

Explore the countryside, your town square or park, and see the patterns in a flurry of leaves, a sudden rainbow breaking through the greyness, or the upward swirling of rooks at bedtime and allow images, words and impressions to form about everything and anything. If you are new to nature divination, spend a week or two, perhaps on holiday or over two or three weekends, really tuning into the sounds, images and impressions of nature. Sit close to a fountain in a park, a waterfall or a river. Listen to rain beating on a roof or wind howling in a chimney. Each has a distinct voice, but some voices you may relate to more easily, so spend extra time asking questions and hearing answers of those you are most in tune with.

Fire Divination

Especially at the great festivals, the way the sacred fires burned would augur the success of the harvests or herds (no doubt wise Druidesses and Druids would build the fires carefully to inspire the maximum optimism and confidence).

You can practise your fire divination on a domestic fire, perhaps created in a small brazier or even using your barbecue coals glistening with fat; garden bonfires with wood smoke are also excellent sources of inspiration. Or you can light a huge candle in your cauldron. Sacrificial fires were considered especially effective for seeking omens. In modern fire divination, you could cast a handful of fragrant herbs on the fire, perhaps those with natural kinship to fire, such as basil, fennel or mint.

It was considered a good omen if a sacrificial fire was clear, the flames transparent rather than dark red or yellow, and if the fire crackled. A fire that burned silently, was difficult to light, blown about by the wind or slow to consume the sacrifice, indicated that the coming days and events were not so propitious.

Powdered pitch was also traditionally thrown on to a fire. If the pitch flared upwards quickly, it augured that the outcome of any action would be favourable. You may prefer to cast pine cones or nuts and see if they crack open or instantly flare up.

Fire Divination for Others

Ask a question and focus on the flames, looking for images within their flickering forms. Answers may come as words in your head, pictures or more subtle feelings or impressions. Again listen to your feelings, and if you feel agitated by the intensity of the flames, move away for a while.

If someone needs advice, ask them to cast a handful of herbs in the fire and then to hold a stick in the flames, being careful that it only chars, while asking the question. Then they should cast the smouldering stick into the flames and, where it flares, an image will appear. Ask the person to name the picture they see in the fire, or the words and images that come into the mind, without pausing to rationalise.

Repeat the ritual with another stick and a new question may emerge spontaneously. Continue until four or five images have been obtained. You can then consider how the symbols together provide a solution to the questions, or offer suggestions for moving on.

You can adapt the ritual using a large candle and long-handled incense sticks that can be lit from the candle as the question is asked. Momentarily hold the incense sticks in the flame and allow them to flare to create an image. Sandalwood, myrrh and frankincense are especially potent.

Cloud Divination

Cloud divination is my own personal favourite. It does take time, but it is no bad thing to withdraw from external stimulation to clear the mind, although you can read the sky quickly for instant input.

Before you begin cloud divination, spend time cloud watching in different places and at different times. Gaze at a dawn sky over the sea. Contemplate clouds on a still afternoon on a hilltop with fluffy clouds barely moving. Scan the fast-scudding clouds over a plain before a storm or on a windy day; observe clouds heavy with snow, sudden small black clouds in an otherwise blue sky, and those sunset, crimson and purple cloud pillows. You can also study white or grey clouds in a night-dark sky.

Another excellent source for modern Druidesses comes from cloud watching from the window of an aircraft. All clouds have different images and associated impressions. Do not force pictures to form, but note any that seem especially significant and the feelings they evoke.

For your first cloud divination, choose a day of fine warm weather when the clouds are quite distinct from one another. Here's how to proceed.

- You should sit or lie on a hilltop or in a field for at least an hour and allow the sky pictures to float along, slowly change and combine.

- Clear your mind of clutter by placing any worries or unfinished business on a passing cloud dragon's tail.

- Allow your body to merge with the grass and the sky, so that you breathe as one in time with the pulse of nature.

- When you are ready, allow a question or area of concern to emerge from deep within you.

- Half close your eyes and focus on a group of clouds, allowing them to create a scene or a series of images. Let these images create feelings, impressions, words. Let the process continue until no more images bubble into your mind.

- Wait while the clouds slowly move and re-form and you may obtain a second picture.

- When you have collected two or three cloud formation images, scribble down all your impressions while they are fresh in your mind. Do not analyse them at the time, as this is a slow-germinating method.

- Walk home or back to your car slowly, by which time the conscious mind will have joined with the psyche to make spontaneous connections.

• You can work with another person who needs to answer a question and interpret the images they identify while you are cloud watching.

Collective Cloud Work

This can be immensely rewarding as a group activity or with two or three trusted friends. It is a very good way of beginning prophecy, by inspired utterances that need not necessarily be about the future, but can shed insight into current issues, whether global or related to the group. It is also a good way of planning a strategy for a joint venture of activity. You will need a tape recorder, as there will be a lot of material to remember. This is what you do.

• Sit on a hilltop or in an open place and face the same bank of clouds. Fast-moving ones are best.

• Choose someone to begin cloud watching and remember that they should keep talking until all their inspiration has been expressed. Get them to identify a cloud, e.g., 'I see a lioness.'

• Do not be afraid to express emotions and impressions such as, 'She is leaving the forest and entering a clearing. She knows she must find others to survive the coming winter.'

• The next person picks another cloud. 'I see a wolf. He has lost the pack because he is running from the hunters. But he feels no regrets, as the others were too slow, too bound in their conventions. He is a lone wolf by nature.'

• When you have finished, play back the recording. Listen in silence. Then toss the ideas between you. Perhaps the cloud impressions symbolise a situation in the world arena, a concern you all have for a local issue, or one that mirrors the uncertainties and decisions you as a group are struggling with. If the symbolism does not become clear, appoint a scribe to write down the new impressions as you collectively analyse the recording scene by scene.

• When you are alone, expand on the story, perhaps setting it to music or writing it in verse, painting the images or sculpting the cloud characters. You may enter the scene in your dreams where the landscape will expand. You can take these insights back to the group.

- If you carry out the exercise every month or so your saga will evolve, reflecting the changing energies in the clouds as the seasons wheel.

- You can also use this method with a family to sort out domestic issues creatively.

Water Divination

Scrying or seeking images in water is the oldest form of divination, practised in dark pools by moonlight or in brilliant sunlight.

Traditionally, water for scrying is darkened with mugwort and worked with in the hour before sunset, so that the natural light on the water becomes increasingly scarlet. You can surround your bowl with pink and purples candles to emulate the effect.

Whether you use a natural pool with shadows cast by trees, passing clouds and natural sources of light, or trees or an indoor water source, illuminated by candles, sunlight or moonlight, scrying involves merging with the reflective substance, that is the water, so that the images from the deep, unconscious parts of your psyche can, as it were, slide on to the surface of the water. Here are some more hints on water divination.

- Burn lavender or rose incense to break down the conscious barriers that keep telling you there is nothing in the water.

- Indoors, arrange candles and sit near a slightly open window so that the surface of the water ripples.

- Floating candles with glass nuggets or small crystals on the bottom of the bowl can be very effective if you are new to water scrying.

- In daylight dispense with the candle and allow sunlight to fall on the water, placing crystals and small mirrors around the bowl so that they amplify spots of radiance on the water.

- Ask your question, stir the water nine times with a twig, close your eyes momentarily, open them and blink. As you stare at the surface, name what comes into your mind, whether it appears externally on the surface of the water or in your mind's eye.

- Stir again nine times and repeat for a second and third image.

- Whether you are alone or reading for someone else, speak aloud quite spontaneously about each image (record what you say as it is easy to forget details) and continue to speak, unless the person for whom you are reading wishes to add their interpretation, based on any personal significance. Then put together the whole picture and relate it to the question.

- Where possible try outdoor scrying in sunlight or moonlight, or illuminate a garden pond with torches. Use a long branch to ripple the water.

Herbs on the Surface of Water

The above method is very powerful, but you may find it easier if you are reading for another person to use clear water and sprinkle dried herbs on the surface, so that there are tangible external focuses from which you can both derive images. It is also a good transitory stage if you find pure water scrying unproductive. You can, of course, use this method for private divination.

- Fill a deep, clear glass bowl slowly from a jug of water until it is just over half-full.

- While the water is still moving, drop on to the surface a few dried culinary herbs, such as herbes de Provence, rosemary, basil or parsley, which have reasonably large, separate leaves.

- These will swirl around, giving an image or maybe several, and if you add the herbs a few at a time you can keep them swirling and see new images forming.

- Again use a tape recorder, as you and the questioner will be calling out many changing forms.

- When the water is still, draw what you can recall of the shapes or write their names all over a piece of paper; allow the questioner to name the key image/s and draw a small circle around them.

- Together draw connecting lines from the other images to the key images, and then between the main images, exploring the inter-connections as you work.

• Tip the divination water away into either soil or running water (a tap and sink will do) so that the energies will continue to flow.

Developing Personal Prophetic Powers

There are some tantalisingly brief accounts in early medieval Irish literature of Druidic rituals to induce prophecy, usually in dreams. A trance-like state was induced in which prophets were made to answer the questions of those present.

Since adaptations of these rituals have become regarded as an effective method of prophecy in modern Druidic practice, I will now describe some of the methods that have filtered down over the centuries.

• A Druid or Druidess would sleep beneath a waterfall wrapped in a bull hide so that the intense sound would flood the consciousness. This seems to be associated with the sacrificing of a bull on the Midwinter festival. With the waterfall, the Druid or Druidess may at first light have been taken from the thick bull hide and pushed into the brilliant water, with the sudden flooding of stimuli perhaps triggering prophecy from the unconscious parts of the mind.

• A Druid or Druidess would sit against a rowan tree, again enclosed within a bull skin.

• A Druid or Druidess would sleep in one of the Neolithic long barrow burial mounds that can still be entered on ancient hilltops in the UK and other parts of Europe. It may be that the Druid or Druidess was woken by the dawn light of the following day, which was allowed to flood into the long barrow, thus creating by the sudden breaking of the darkness and sensory deprivation a heightened awareness of the future. This is certainly not for the faint-hearted.

Modern Sensory Techniques

There are gentler ways of contrasting the sensations, darkness and stillness, to access the more inspired reaches of our psyche. If you are going to work in a wild or lonely place, take a trusted friend or family member or another Druidess to guide and protect you, not only from human predators but also from the fears and loneliness such moments can bring. Gentle techniques are more effective and much safer than harsh deprivations, for which modern life has ill prepared us. Leaping into freezing waterfalls may not be the best option when we have flotation tanks available.

What will you see and say? Who knows? These special times may inspire poetry, a book, creating a modern mythological or Tolkien-type work; perhaps you may have insights into world situations, into family or work matters, or awareness of receiving messages from your guardian, or perhaps a being of light who teaches you many things. Some of this wisdom you may record; some you may keep in your heart. You will see only what it is wise for you to see – certainly not a gloomy foretelling of doom, but of pathways towards what should be fulfilling avenues. Here are some suggestions for your consideration.

- As mentioned above, try working in a flotation tank. These are part of many alternative health centres and are very safe because the saline water is so concentrated that even if you fall asleep, which many people do, you cannot sink. You can ask for lights to be switched on ten minutes before the end of the session to allow you to formulate and work with your visions in the protected environment.

- Alternatively, camp on a wet weekend either in your garden or in a forest camping ground. Set the tent where no artificial light will shine and listen to the rain beating on it. Or rent a small chalet on a very quiet site near a river or waterfall, or next to the sea, where you hear the sound of rushing or surging water all night long. In your mind flow with the water and do not try to sleep unless it comes naturally, in which case you may experience prophetic dreams.

- Massive megalithic stone chambers with earth mounds above them or long barrows provide darkness and silence, and many can still be visited. However, because the energies are so powerful, you would need no more than five minutes sitting in the darkness for quite powerful feelings to come. Indeed, more would be unwise. Again, go with a friend, someone with their feet on the ground, who will empathise with your experiences, but prevent you wandering off psychically.

• Caves are another good source of stillness and darkness, and some are still totally untouched, especially those on seashores. Check tide times carefully and have an alarm set in case you drift off for too long. If possible work on a dull or misty day.

In the following chapter we will look at what has become the hallmark of Druidic divination and prophecy, the tree staves representing the Celtic holy trees.

7

Becoming a Tree Mother

I have written about trees a number of times in this book, because trees are to me the uniting thread that runs through the evolving spirituality of a Druidess. In this chapter we will look at what are considered the traditional Celtic trees.

In 1948, the scholar and historian Robert Graves recreated the *Tree Alphabet* from his interpretation of the Celtic poem, *Cad Goddeu* (The Battle of the Trees), which was attributed to the sixth-century bard Taliesin. He also studied medieval Celtic texts that are claimed to be based on copies of earlier works, recorded perhaps as early as the tenth century, but since these were lost this cannot be verified.

There is some traditional material on the use of Celtic trees from Ireland and Scotland, although this is not contemporaneous to the Celts. For example, the fourteenth-century *Book of Ballymote* from County Silog, said to be a copy of a ninth-century work, tells how the God Ogma (Sun Face) created the ogham alphabet. Other sources of knowledge about ogham come from the seventeenth-century Scottish *Scholar's Primer*, which recorded the oral usage, while in Ireland O'Flaherty's *Ogygia* was published in 1793.

Many of the modern systems of tree divination draw heavily on Robert Graves's interpretations. These give us at least some key to special trees that grew in the forests of Europe, until many were cut down during the Middle Ages for farmland. Although I do work with the tree alphabet and you can read about my system in *A Complete Guide to Divination*, I have found that direct visualisation of the Tree Mothers is for women perhaps the single most important spiritual step in becoming a wise Druidess.

The magical meanings I have used for the trees are ones that have filtered through Celtic myths and folklore, as well as being gleaned from Graves's interpretations. They are accepted by a number of modern Druid orders.

Who Are the Tree Mothers?

For me, the most important part of my work as a solitary Druidess has been discovering the Tree Mothers. In German and Swedish folklore, there are still references to the Hylder, Holder or Tree Mothers of the elder tree. From England comes the tale of the Elder Mother whose tree was close to the Rollright Stones, ancient standing stones in Oxfordshire. In legend these stones have been identified as an invading king and his army who, at an unspecified period in history, were turned to stone by the old Hag or Elder Mother of Rollright. She thereafter lived in an elder tree close to the stones to stand sentinel throughout the centuries in case the enchantment was broken.

On Midsummer Eve right until the Second World War, accounts tell of locals who would go to the King Stone and after a feast would ceremonially cut the elder tree, which then bled (originally it was believed to bring fertility to the land). The tree has since been cut down, but there are signs of regrowth and there is still an active pagan community that carries out rituals at the stones.

Other tree spirit matriarchs were recognised as Goddesses and given Goddess names in Celtic folklore. There is Druantia, in the Orkney Isles, the Silver Fir Goddess, sometimes called by modern Druidesses the Mother of the Tree Alphabet and Divination. In Gaul she was associated also with the Oak Mother, wise, authoritative and highly prophetic. More shadowy and elusive is Nemetona or Nemain, a goddess from Gaul who has survived in folklore. Some modern practitioners called her Mother of the Sacred Groves – she may speak from any tree or her form may suddenly appear in a momentary flurry as the wind lifts and scatters a pile of autumn leaves.

Modern Druidesses have identified other Tree Mothers as a focus of mature wisdom that even the youngest woman working as a Druidess can acquire by working with trees. Although I have focused on Celtic-associated trees, many of which actually flourish in other parts of the world, by using the methods I suggest you will probably be able to identify Tree Mothers in your own indigenous trees whose characteristics may seem to you to mirror those I have identified in my work as a Druidess and folklorist.

The Tree Mothers are worth getting to know. They are more helpful to new Druidesses and Druids than the younger dryad tree spirits you can catch out of the corner of your eye flitting about, who have not lived through the experiences of the Tree Mothers. The Tree Mothers are usually found in older trees, gnarled ones with quite distinctive features on the trunk. Very old ones are Tree Grandmothers.

The Tree Mothers are immensely comforting, protective in cold, lonely times, but challenging, too, like any tough mother pushing her reluctant offspring to ever greater achievements personally and spiritually. Each offers the qualities of her own tree species and the wisdom of the ages through which she has lived, which may be very many, for she may have moved to different trees over the centuries.

Identifying Tree Mothers

To find a Tree Mother, visit a mature forest or piece of ancient woodland. There may be a number of Tree Mothers there, belonging to the same species, for they are all sisters. They are bonded in the need to housekeep the wooded places and to ensure that we do not kill off the lungs of the world.

You may identify a Tree Mother most easily in a tree that is coiled, with many offshoots – even in a slender species with branches or leaves that wind around you, but not in a menacing way. If you sit against one of these trees, look for a hole near one of the roots and in your mind's vision enter and go down the winding tunnels; it could be like an Alice in Wonderland type rabbit hole, or more orderly, with steps. There you will meet the Tree Mother and maybe some of her Sisters who have come to visit, busy, bustling, kindly, reminding you of what needs to be finished and mended in your life. Don't expect to sit and have a meaningful discussion about the nature of the universe – you will be given your list of chores and sent off home with a cake. It is rather like visiting an elderly aunt's home when she is spring-cleaning or entertaining her equally daunting friends.

You may have a doctorate in nuclear physics and control a budget of millions in the workaday world, but to any Tree Mother you are just like a troublesome, though well-loved, five-year-old girl. In time, as you enter the world of the roots, you will be allowed to listen to the wisdom of the Tree Mothers as they stir their cauldrons and weave fate from the fronds of the forest, and as you sleep and when you are afraid, you will feel the protection of the Tree Mother with whom you most resonate or whose qualities you need. She will not usurp the role of your special guide but will teach you different things. If you are very lucky, a Tree Mother may even foster you and become your special guide.

Below I have listed the qualities I have discovered in the Tree Mothers of the Celtic trees, but your encounters may be different.

If you live in non-Celtic lands, you will, as I said, still find Tree Mothers in the olive, the date palm, the orange tree or the banyan and many other tropical trees that mature much earlier in warm climes – or in the trees and bushes of the far north. They will reflect the climate and the soil that nurtures those trees, and so your Mediterranean or Californian Mother may be alternately fiery and expansive. In contrast your Mother of the northern Steppes will have little time for pleasantries as she struggles to protect her roots from the ice and snow, but she may uphold you in the most drear and dire situations.

Becoming Tree-wise

As I said when talking about the sacred grove, unless you are already an expert in identifying trees, take along a good tree book in your crane bag when you go out into the countryside. Arboretums are an excellent starting point for the novice tree-seeker, as are botanical gardens, because the species are often well and accurately labelled; there is far more variety than you would find in modern woodland. Such knowledge takes years to acquire, but it is very worth while doing so. In fact, becoming a tree detective can appeal to even the most world-weary adolescent.

Unlike our forebears who walked through forests every day that were home to a relatively limited number of species, today even country dwellers have less continuous access to nature; because of the increase in communication and international botanical cross-pollenisation, many varieties of tree and bush grow in areas perhaps thousands of miles from their places of origin. Even if you use a really good tree book, the growing species can look nothing like the picture. So take a series of small, waterproof bags and sticky labels in your crane bag, plus the all-essential pens and pencils.

Pick a small sprig to give the leaf formation, gather any berries, etc., and if possible take a small fallen twig, so you can look at the bark at leisure. All of this will not only tell you who is talking to you, but will give you a great deal more background knowledge. When you visualise your protective rowan while travelling late on, for example, the London Underground, you will be able to *feel* the bark and the squashy fragrant berries, and see the colour of the leaves, and so join psychically with the tree you saw in Kew Gardens a month before.

Listening to the Leaves

You will already be familiar with the voice of your grove. But if you visit a large expanse of trees or an arboretum you will find that many species put their voices together like a well-tuned choir. This is how to listen to the leaves.

- First attune yourself to the time scale of the wind's natural dialogue with the trees – the wind gusting, catching up the leaves as they dance suspended on their branches, then the silence as the leaves wait in anticipation.

- Before asking a question, tune in to the rhythms of the voice of the leaves, which may speak in a lilt, in a staccato manner or in a rush like a wave crashing on the shore. When you are attuned, cast your question into the waiting silence and allow it to be first taken up by the wind, which may have answers of her own, adding to the wisdom of the echoing leaves.

- Ask a second question, then a third, and afterwards allow the leaves to add anything that is unsaid as the wind catches them once more.

- Find a sheltered spot to scribble down what may be a series of seemingly unconnected words or a theme in which one word recurs, for example *wait* or *seek* or *forgive.*

• When you return home, arrange or rearrange the phrases and you may find they relate not only to the questions asked, but also to more general issues, or suggest a way that your life might progress.

• You may find that different trees are good for different issues relating to their essential nature, for example the oak for matters of the future, the hazel for issues concerning justice or learning, and the yew for core issues of life, death and immortality.

The Message of the Tree Mothers

I have provided a symbol for each of the twenty Tree Mothers listed on the following pages. These are the most authenticated tree associations used in modern tree divination. You can draw the symbols on wooden discs or twigs and focus on one while visualising a particular Tree Mother when you are indoors. You could also paint the symbols on the relevant crystals and carry one with you to work or when you go out, to help you to draw the symbolic qualities you need into your mind. The crystal associations are modern so you may feel that other crystals resonate better then the ones suggested. When you work with the Tree Mothers, you could burn a candle in their special colour, or the herb as incense.

You will probably find that one of the Tree Mothers will become your special guardian and will visit you in dreams or moments of quiet reverie. Each Tree Mother may develop a distinctive voice in your mind's ear. As you work with them you will build up your own image of each Tree Mother, so I have only given you an outline in the list below. Record your own images in your journal.

If you are uncertain about a course of action, or face a particularly challenging day ahead, you can put all your Tree Mother symbols in a drawstring bag made of a natural fabric. Draw one out at random and you will find that the symbol indicates the Tree Mother who can best help you; carry her symbol with you. I have given the names, used by Graves, that on the whole are those used in Druidry for what are called the sacred trees.

The ivy, fern, heather, gorse and vine are bushes. They were included by Graves in his *Tree Alphabet* because they were mentioned in the Celtic poem *Cad Goddeu* and so have become associated with tree powers. If you find it hard to imagine their ruling mother, you can leave them out. I have described how I see them in the following section.

List of Celtic Tree Mothers

The names used by Graves are listed first, followed by the name in common use, with the Latin name in parentheses. The order given is that established for the *Tree Alphabet*.

Beith/Birch (Betula pendula)

The birch is magically symbolic of rebirth.

The Birch Mother is most often seen in the person of her Daughter, the Maiden of Spring, and she will fill you with enthusiasm and an eagerness to be moving. But the Mother is the one who can help you to clear up your life when all seems chaotic or spoiled; her tough love will help to push you out to try again.

Colour   White.

Herb   Rosemary.

Crystal   Clear quartz/red sard.

Her message is that there is much that you need to explore within yourself, thereby bringing positive change and innovation to all aspects of your world.

Luis/Rowan or Mountain Ash (Sorbus acuparia)

The rowan has become associated in magic and folk tradition with protection and the Moon.

The Rowan Mother is a natural healer, seen best in moonlight, brewing potions especially with rowan berries, to heal all ills and to bring long life. She is especially kind to those who have suffered abuse of any kind and will pass on her healing powers if you open your heart to love for your fellow creatures, even those not worthy of it.

Colour   Grey.

Herb   Thyme.

Crystal   Yellow cat's eye/tourmaline.

Her message is that you possess inner resources that can enable you to avoid danger and turn obstacles to advantage, if you listen to your inner voice.

Fearn/Alder (Alnus glutinosa)

 The alder is a tree associated in Celtic myths with the power of fire and of personal sacrifice.

The Alder Mother is no stranger to sacrifice and offers a safe base from which to further essentially practical and useful ventures, rather than personal quests for glory. She advocates patience, and if you have been hurt emotionally helps you to learn to trust again slowly. Her fire is slow burning and will warm you emotionally if you feel drained of energy and hope.

Herb   Basil.

Colour   Crimson.

Crystal   Blue beryl/aquamarine.

Her message is that you can turn your dreams into reality if you keep your feet on the ground even if your head is in the stars.

Saille/Willow (Salix alba)

 In folklore the willow is a tree of the Moon and of intuitive wisdom.

The Willow Mother has great empathy with others and so suffers the pain of every injured bird or trampled flower; she will teach you to see into the hearts of others. This gift makes you a wise counsellor and diviner, but also makes you more open to suffering on behalf of others.

Colour   The colour of fire/silvery grey.

Herb   Poppy.

Crystal   Moonstone/fire opal.

Her message is that you should trust your intuitions and your dreams, whether in matters of the heart, your working world or your psychic explorations.

Nunn/Ash (Farinas excelsior)

   The ash is a tree of noble intentions and integrity.

The Ash Mother is equally stately and demands always that we seek the greatest good and apply the highest standards in whatever we do; the good of others is her motto. She also encourages us towards quiet leadership and to pass on teaching our Druidic insights and respect for the environment to the next generation.

Colour   Bright green.

Herb   Sage.

Crystal   Garnet/carnelian.

Her message is that we cannot compromise what we know to be important, but that we must be tolerant towards others who lack vision.

Huathe/Hawthorn or Whitethorn (Crataegus oxacantha)

The hawthorn is a tree associated with fertility and with the coming of summer, emotionally as well as in fact.

The Hawthorn Mother rejoices at her daughter in her white finery, still seen today in May Day processions in the form of the young May Queen. But she turns her own face to the winds and storms that can arise at any time; she is the Mother who urges us on but gives us her own cloak so we will be protected from the squalls.

Colour   Purple.

Herb   Chives.

Crystal   Lapis lazuli.

Her message is that we must not lose courage in our quest to create a better world, but that sometimes we do need to withdraw spiritually to become strong.

Duir/English and Sessile Oak (**Quercus robur/alba**)

The oak has come to symbolise the mature wisdom of the Druid or Druidess, gained through experience and intensive prolonged study of the natural world.

The Oak Mother is the Arch Druidess of the trees who will seem always to be teaching, a remote headmistress figure who nevertheless occasionally reveals an acute knowledge of the real world and the foibles of her less attentive pupils. She is the one who demands that we spend those extra minutes whether in divination or in contemplation after ritual to understand more fully the experience and insights gained.

Colour   Black or dark brown.

Herb   St John's wort.

Crystal   White sapphire/sunstone.

Her message is that there are no short cuts to wisdom, and that all life, good and bad, is a learning experience.

Tinne/Holly (Ilex aquifolium)

In Celtic myth the holly is a powerful animus or male symbol of the sexual potency of the leader and also of the struggle for dominance.

The Holly Mother is also strongly combative, challenging injustice and demanding that due respect be given to all creation; she is not a lady who will tolerate litter in her grove. She reminds us that at times a Druidess does need to be assertive, although not aggressive and fierce, in defending those who are vulnerable.

Colour   Dark grey.

Herb   Aconite (monk's hood).

Crystal   Ruby/citrine.

Her message is that we should not deny the vital shadow aspects of ourselves, but transform what is negative into power for positive change.

Coll/Hazel (Corylus avellana)

The hazel is magically a symbol of tradition, justice and order.

The Hazel Mother is the Mother slowest to anger, whose melodious voice soothes the troubled into sleep and whose advice hidden in puzzles enables her children to solve their seeming insoluble dilemmas creatively and harmoniously. She is also amazingly fertile and nurturing, so none are hungry or cold in her dwelling, but all carry away with them the responsibility for likewise offering hospitality to all.

Colour   Brown.

Herb   Kelp.

Crystal   Banded red agate/topaz.

Her message is to resist emotional swings and to recognise that those who differ from us may nevertheless have valid viewpoints.

Quert/Apple (**Malus sylvestris,** *the Crab Apple*)

 The apple has become, through medieval myths of the old Celtic stories, the symbol of the Tree of Life, of abundance and of immortality.

The Apple Mother has a groaning table and a bubbling cauldron and talks constantly as she works, surrounded by babies and small animals, restoring youth to the aged, health to the ailing, strength to the weak and love to the lonely, in a constant interchange of energies. You may have little chance to commune alone with her, but you will learn all kinds of important lessons about sharing abundance and giving freely of time and energy, in return being energised and revitalised.

Colour   Tawny coloured or green.

Herb   Strawberry/rose.

Crystal   Rose quartz/emerald.

Her message is give freely of your time and energy and you will in return gain abundant spiritual wealth.

Muin/Vine (**Vitis vinifera**)

The vine has become a symbol of intense joy and total involvement in life.

The Vine Mother is not at all uncontrolled in her joy; for she knows that great joy is balanced on the cosmic see-saw with great sorrow. So she drinks deeply from the cup of happiness, but meets our eyes, telling us silently we must not forget the price we sometimes pay for following our hearts and giving everything. Visualise her tall and swaying upwards towards the Sun, balancing a jug of wine on her head.

Colour   Mixed shades of green.

Herb   Mint.

Crystal   Amethyst.

Her message is that only if we are truly happy with ourselves can we bring happiness to others.

Gort/Ivy (Hedera helix)

Ivy as an evergreen and binding plant became symbolised in magic with committed love and fidelity, and with a safe, secure home environment.

The Ivy Mother is a very bustling matriarch, arranging and rearranging, and insisting on the importance of keeping commitments, and of fidelity to principles as well as people. She talks of the essential delicate balance of different aspects of the self, of self and others, of nurturing versus self-reliance, dependence and independence, all issues we must resolve if we are to be individuals and yet love and be loved. Visualise her as a well-endowed medieval housewife dressed in green.

Colour   Sky blue.

Herb   Honeysuckle.

Crystal   Yellow serpentine/rutilated quartz.

Her message is that the most binding ties are not those where emotional blackmail or vulnerability are exploited, but those based on free choice and free will.

Ngetal Ferns/Bracken (Pteridum aquilinum)

Ferns are associated magically with prosperity and hidden wealth.

The Fern Mother is surrounded by riches, but they are all spiritual gifts: peace of mind, contentment at home and work, quiet sleep, the love and respect of others – all of which cannot be bought with earthly gold, but must be won by spiritual endeavour. She reminds us that health and good luck come from the bounty of the Mother and so should be highly prized and used to help others.

Colour   Grass green and gold.

Herb   Fennel.

Crystal   Green jasper/sapphire.

Her message is that we should seek to develop our hidden talents so that we can repay the cosmos for the blessings we receive.

Straif/Blackthorn (**Rhamnus catharticus**)

 The blackthorn has come magically and in myth to represent strength under duress and sudden moments of joy even in dark times.

The Blackthorn Mother is, except for the Yew Mother, older and more careworn than all the others, having lost count of the numerous wandering souls she has rescued who have got out of their depth in life and spirituality. If you are sad or alone, she will spend time with you, her hands more gentle than those of any Maiden Goddess, and if you look into her eyes you will lose many fears of ageing, mortality and the ultimate solitude of the human condition – you will understand the enduring beauty of wisdom and experience.

Colour   Dark blue.

Herb   Hyssop.

Crystal   Jet/obsidian.

Her message is that there may not be an ideal time for us to begin a venture, so we should persevere even in less than ideal circumstances.

Ruis/Elder (**Sambucus canadensis**)

 The elder is, in medieval Celtic myth, the ultimate fairy tree and a source of magical wisdom.

The Elder Mother is very wise and versed in all the Druidic arts, especially healing. But she is a demanding Mother, returning a question with a more challenging question. She shows us the places where we may go and find the answers for ourselves, sometimes by routes where we confront shadows of the self on the way.

Colour   Blood red.

Herb   Juniper.

Crystal   Malachite/peridot.

Her message is that you should look for magical inspiration in the everyday world and not just your spiritual work.

Ailim/Pine or Silver Fir (*Pinaceae*/**Abies alba**)

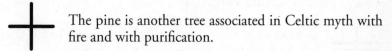

The pine is another tree associated in Celtic myth with fire and with purification.

The Fir Mother, silvered and beautiful, is fierce in protection of the weak, but her blazing torches can demand that we cleanse ourselves of old prejudices, illusions and bitterness before opening up to learn the secrets of ritual at her hearth.

Colour   Light blue or piebald.

Herb   Cowslip.

Crystal   Haematite.

Her message is to seek to purify your spiritual work from the ego and power trips that are all too common among spiritual gurus.

Onn/Furze or Gorse (**Ulex europaeus**)

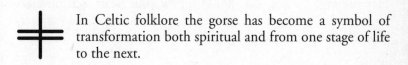

In Celtic folklore the gorse has become a symbol of transformation both spiritual and from one stage of life to the next.

The Gorse Mother is not as prickly as might be expected, but she is a natural spring cleaner, transforming the somewhat dusty material she is given into something shining new. So expect a lot of intensive input. Some insights may be unwelcome, but a definite reordering and redirecting will take place, so that you leave with your head whirling but full of determination. Visualise her as an angular woman farmer, wearing what seems to be a blaze of golden rays.

Colour   Yellow gold and silver.

Herb   Lavender.

Crystal   Iron pyrites.

Her message is that all experiences, good and bad, can be transformed into wisdom to guide our future path.

Ur/Heather (Calluna vulgaris)

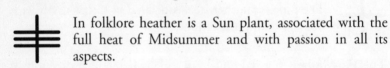 In folklore heather is a Sun plant, associated with the full heat of Midsummer and with passion in all its aspects.

The Heather Mother is a Mother of the Sun, powerfully creative, energising, found always outdoors in a patch of sunlight. She will expect you to work as you talk, to complete her many tasks necessary to keep the wheel turning. Stay close and you will be filled with a little of her light and creativity. Visualise her as a radiant woman dressed in scarlet and purple striding across moorland in the noonday Sun.

Colour   Scarlet and purple.

Herb   Marigold.

Crystal   Amber.

Her message is that you should follow your heart, seizing every moment of happiness, for opportunities do not come along every day.

Eadha/White Poplar (Populus alba)

 In Celtic myth the white poplar has become associated with the later years of life and with gentle, gradual healing.

The Poplar Mother may seem very slight and quiet, but within her crane bag she holds many secrets that you will need to understand. Sit very quietly with her, sometimes straining to hear her whispered wisdom; she can heal aspects of your life that you have never revealed and will do so unobtrusively, so you are just aware of heavy burdens lifted.

Colour Silver white.

Herb Chamomile.

Crystal Fluorite.

Her message is let the past go and make peace within yourself, if others will not accept reconciliation.

Ido or Ioho/Yew (**Taxus baccata**)

 The yew has become associated with endings, leading to new beginnings. Yew spikes are poisonous, however, so you should be very careful how you handle this tree and its leaves.

The Yew Mother sits alone in her dark cloak, her face half-hidden, and it takes courage to approach her. But creep close and she will enfold you in silence, telling you things in your soul you may not understand for many years, no matter how old or wise you are. But you will be aware that your life has been touched by grace and by blessing. Look beyond her and you will see the Birch Mother waiting, and so the cycle begins anew.

Colour Dark green.

Herb Cypress.

Crystal Bloodstone.

Her message is do not be afraid to let go of what is no longer positive or fulfilling in your life.

In the next chapter we will take what we have learned from these wise Mothers and apply it to healing ourselves, those we love and the planet itself.

8

Herbal Healing

Women are natural healers. A mother knows instinctively how to soothe a child's headache or fretfulness and many women, mothers or not, seem to be able to use their voices to soothe the pain or mental anguish of those with whom they share a close relationship. This may occur because a psychic link with a person triggers into action the immune system, which science is increasingly recognising is affected by spiritual and emotional processes.

The Healing Cauldron of the Druidesses

Although we have virtually no historical material on Druidesses healing from Celtic times, descriptions of female healing deities with their magical cauldrons have come down through the medieval stories and folklore of the Celtic world. One theory is that these goddesses may have been actual healers whose fame transformed them in folktales into deities who, according to popular Celtic myth, mingled freely with mortals.

Becoming a Healer

What is important is that modern Druidesses do seem to find that their innate healing powers increase spontaneously or perhaps appear for the first time as they work with Sun power or the energies of the trees in their Druidic work. Indeed, you may find that as you spend time in the open air, your fingertips will become sensitised, and you may even become aware of faint golden sparks of energy shimmering around them. If you touch, for example, a friend's aching shoulder soon after you have been working spiritually, your friend may express surprise at feeling a mild but pleasant tingling, and will usually comment that the pain is at least temporarily eased. Over the months and years, you will find that your success rate and the permanence of cure improves as your Druidic wisdom increases.

For some women this healing power becomes part of their everyday world. You may be satisfied to use this enhanced healing wisdom in your daily life for spontaneous touches or sympathetic words that relieve or cure another's emotional hurt.

Herbs and Druidesses

A number of modern Druidesses work with herbs, feeling instinctively that Druidesses in history likewise healed their communities using herbs, although they did not record their wisdom, so that we cannot refer directly to a Druid herbal.

However, over the centuries women have brewed herbs or applied them as poultices, and some of us have herbal remedies handed down by our great-great-grandmothers that have come from their own great-great-grandmothers. Therefore it would not take too great a leap of imagination to believe that Druidesses, with their long training, would have been at least as skilled in their arts as the late medieval wise woman healers.

These latter women came to our attention as victims of the witchcraft trials from the early fifteenth to the late seventeenth centuries. Indeed, I am not the only Druidess to speculate that after Druidry was forbidden or replaced by Celtic Christianity, a number of Druidesses went to live in villages, and then made their living as healers and midwives. It can also be hypothesised that the reputation of Celtic Christian convents and abbeys, especially in Ireland, as centres of healing and herbcraft excellence, may owe at least something to the conversion of Druidess and indeed Druid healers.

Of course herbal work today is very different from when our ancestors went out into the forests and fields and used herbs that grew in their own region, becoming through direct teaching of older family members familiar not only with the plants, but also their medical uses and the correct dosage, and which herbs or parts of herbs were poisonous. Today, especially in towns, we can find few herbs growing wild that are unpolluted, but we can buy from herbalists and by mail order a bewildering array of herbs from around the world. Although we potentially have a wider range of products, we do not grow up with them as part of our daily lives.

True medicinal herbcraft is a skilled art and I have suggested a number of books from which you can acquire basic knowledge about how to make herbal brews, which herbs should not be used in pregnancy or with certain medical conditions, and how to make herbal remedies for a variety of ailments. Such knowledge can be very useful in your work as a healer, and if you do have a friendly herbal pharmacy you can gain much information here and also from courses run by qualified herbalists. Even local colleges of education are increasingly offering evening classes in these ancient traditions.

Moreover, if you carry a herb book with you on days out in the countryside or to garden centres, you can learn to identify important herbs and in time create your own herb garden of important healing herbs. If you live in a flat you can set up a window box or indoor shelf at home of herbs you particularly value. Many herbs, whether dried or growing, have properties that protect a home and its inhabitants psychically. I have mentioned these properties in the list of herbs.

Spiritual Herbalism

Healing with herbs can also be a magical, spiritual process. Indeed, some modern Druidesses, myself included, would argue that the most important way of transferring healing properties psychically to patients is by practising spiritual herbalism without worrying about dosages and whether a herb may react adversely on an individual's physical system. The method is also very effective for healing people or animals that are absent, and endangered species or polluted places. This is the aspect of Druidic healing on which I am concentrating – channelling higher energies and infusing herbs with magical healing properties that can improve health and well-being from the spirit and thereby through the whole person. This separates spiritual healing from pure aromatherapy or herbalism, although both are very valuable.

A Healing Focus

As a Druidess you can heal in the name of any deity whom you revere – in the name of God, the Goddess or a more abstract power of goodness and light. A number of Druidesses and Druids find the Celtic Goddess Airmid, the Irish healing goddess of medicinal plants, a powerful focus for their healing work.

Stories about Airmid say that she was the daughter of the God of Medicine, Diancecht. After the death of her brother Miach (a hint maybe that she was a mortal Druidess healer), Airmid cared for his grave, on which all the herbs of the world grew. As she cut them each described its healing properties.

Cerridwen is another popular healing focus for modern Druidesses (*see page 163*). So is the Irish Brighid, a very popular icon among modern Druidesses, after whom many healing wells dedicated to St Bridget may have originally been named (*see page 163*). Read through the list on pages 161–6 to find a focus that feels right for you.

To focus my healing, I visualise a wise old Druidess stirring a cauldron in her forest dwelling, and in my mind's vision I move closer and closer until my hands become her hands and I can share psychically of her wisdom.

How to Begin Spiritual Herbalism

This is a method I use as part of my Druidic work. It seems to accord well with the ideal of the wise healing Druidess.

The method involves first casting away what is no longer needed in your life or that of your patient, using cleansing herbs, whether for illness in a specific part of your body, guilt or sorrow, and then taking into yourself or the person, animal or place you are healing, the powers that are needed to attract health or well-being, whether strength, courage or specific healing to a particular part of the body.

The combination of magically charged herbs and higher healing energies drawn from the source of light, God/Goddess or Celtic deity focus, seems, by connections we don't yet understand, to trigger the physical and emotional immune system for self-healing.

This is what you will need.

- A small ceramic or iron pot/cauldron that you can fill with water and into which you can drop cleansing herbs to represent what it is you wish to cast away. This you can heat on your stove or outdoors on a spirit/camping gas burner. If you are in the office, you can improvise and split a herbal tea bag in a cup of hot water, visualising your magical cauldron.

- A mortar and pestle, bought either from a kitchen shop or by mail order. Grinding chopped, fresh herbs or dried leaves, bark, roots and flowers can be incredibly therapeutic in itself, and the rhythm allows you to create a powerful healing chant.

- Small purses or squares of natural fabric and cord with which to tie the herbs in a sachet.

- A selection of dried herbs, bark and flowers, etc., in dark glass or ceramic jars with lids (old coffee jars are excellent containers). You can also buy ready-prepared fresh herbs or grow your own. You do not need very many as some, such as lavender or chamomile, are effective in many areas of healing.

You can carry out healing rituals alone for yourself, or for those who are absent using a symbol or photograph. Alternatively, you can work with friends, family or your group, and each can channel individual energies into the herbs by taking turns to mix and stir them, endowing personal healing wishes and empowerments as they stir.

You can work privately with someone who is distressed or anxious. This can be very helpful, for example, in the case of a child who may feel helpless in the face of bullying, if that child physically casts away fear through the herbs and absorbs courage. You can also carry out a ritual to help an endangered species or war-torn land by focusing on a picture.

The Ritual

You prepare the herbs for healing in the following way.

- Select the herbs you will use, one kind for cleansing and

removing pain or sorrow, and one for empowering and healing (*see the list on pages 130–7*).

- Prepare your pot by half-filling it with water. If you do not have the time or setting to boil water, use a large candle wedged in sand in the pot and burn a few grains of the cleansing herb in the flame. Do not light the candle or fire source yet.

- Place your cleansing herbs in an open dish and on them sprinkle a few grains of salt, saying, 'Blessings be. Take away sorrow, take away pain, take away sickness, make whole again.'

- Put your healing herbs in the mortar or use a ceramic mixing bowl and small potato masher or spoon.

- Sit quietly before you begin and light beeswax or pure white candles if working after dark. If possible, work in the open air, lighting garden torches scented with lavender or sandalwood. Place the two containers of herbs in front of you as you work.

- Ask in your own words that higher powers of healing may enter your fingers and state that you work only for the greatest good to heal – you can name the person or place in need of healing. If healing absently, put the symbol or picture where light shines, whether from the Sun, Moon or a candle.

- Visualise or describe aloud to your patient rays of golden light pouring in through the crown of your head, passing down through your brow and your throat energy centres, and flowing thence into your heart, the spiritual energy centre that controls your arms and hands, the instruments of healing. You may experience a tingling in your fingers.

- Point the fingers of both your hands downwards over the cleansing herbs, saying, 'Blessings be; may love, light, life and loveliness flow, sorrows go.'

- Now begin to pound the healing herbs, visualising still light pouring through your fingers into the herbs, and chanting the purpose of the herbs and their names, for example, 'Fennel, fennel, bring courage, courage be, blessings see.'

- Chant slowly, rhythmically and quietly, visualising the light growing ever more bright, like an aura of gold around the healing herbs.

- You will know when the herbs are ready by a sudden flash of radiance and by an awareness that your fingers are feeling warm and that the energy is slowing. The job is done.

Sending the Healing

As I said earlier, Druidic ritual is not like conventional magic in that it does not increase in speed and intensity, rising to a climax, but is more subtle, more even in tempo, and thus perhaps more enduring. When the healing herbs are ready, reduce your chant to a whisper until it fades into silence.

- Light the cauldron or candle, asking the blessings of sacred fire. As it heats talk quietly, whether alone or with others, of better times and brighter days. You will find that words flow – the right words for the occasion with no prompting or planning. The power of the voice, gentle but sure, is a great healer in itself.

- When the water is warm, ask the person to be healed to add the cleansing herbs to the water a few at a time or add them yourself. Ask that pain, sorrow, fear and a specific area of discomfort or general illness be relieved or taken away. If you are healing an absent person or place visualise them on the surface of the water, well and strong.

- After each handful of herbs is added stir the cauldron or ask the patient to do it, being careful to help children or anyone who is frail, saying as it is stirred, 'Go in peace, sorrows [or pain] cease. Come no more, I close the door on [name the worst aspect].'

- When the herbs have disintegrated, turn the heat right down; take the empowered healing herbs and wrap them in a cloth, fold it and tie it at the top with three knots. Alternatively, place the herbs in a purse and hold the sealed container briefly over the cauldron steam, saying, 'Take only what is good and of worth from the past and move to the future through this moment of healing.'

- Put down the purse, extinguish the cauldron and very carefully take three drops from it in a spoon, one at a time. Cast each drop on to the ground to be absorbed by Mother Earth. You can drop them into a special bowl to be disposed of later if you are working on carpet or delicate flooring, or sprinkle them around the symbol or picture.

- Hold the purse or cloth of herbs downwards to the earth, upwards to the sky and either once more over the cooling waters of the cauldron or, if you are using a candle, over a bowl of water you have filled in advance. These directions represent the three realms of the Druidic world, Earth, Sky and Sea.

- Say as you do so, 'Earth, Sky and Sea, add your powers of healing, strength and restoration, new life, light and the flowing of love and harmony.'

- Pour away any excess liquid from the cauldron in a safe place, as even a gentle brew may be toxic for young children or animals.

- Give the herb sachet to the person who needs healing (this may be yourself), or send it to the sick or unhappy person if they would appreciate it; alternatively wrap it in silk with the symbol and keep it in a drawer until the herbs lose their fragrance. If necessary you can repeat the ritual.

How to Choose and Use Herbs

The majority of the herbs used in magic and healing grew in Western Europe, according to sources such as descriptions of Roman colonial gardens in England and France during the first and second century AD. These herbs are also obtainable in other parts of the world. However, you can use herbs that are native to your own region that have similar properties.

Some Druidic plants have toxic parts and so are not listed here, although they may be used in ritual in other parts of the book. For example, mistletoe, the all-healer, is the most magical of Druidic plants, referred to by the Roman chronicler Pliny (*see page 195*) and has many valuable healing uses in modern medicine, but the berries are very poisonous if eaten. In Chapter 5 I have used mistletoe as part of a Moon rite, rather than as a herb *per se*.

All the herbs suggested on pages 130–7 are used medicinally, working with the parts I have suggested for magic use. As you learn more about properties and quantities, you can become the wise woman of your particular 'village', which may consist of friends, family, colleagues and acquaintances.

Magically, you can choose a herb with a general meaning and in your empowerment make it specific. So, for example, a herb such as angelica that protects against attack, can be used for bullying or anxieties about bullying, and to repel office gossip, spiteful neighbours or fears of confrontation. Such fears can have not only mental but also physical consequences, ranging from sleeplessness to migraines and stress-related disorders. So look at the whole question and the whole person, whether using your herbs purely magically or with extra knowledge therapeutically.

Using Herbs in Ritual

For magical purposes, many of these herbs are also available as incenses or essential oils. If you prefer to burn oils or incenses you can first burn away an old sorrow or illness with a cleansing incense/oil, then light a new one for healing. On page 200 I have listed books on aromatherapy that may be helpful if you want to apply essential oils medicinally.

Other Ways of Using Herbs Magically

- You can empower pots or bunches of fresh herbs by placing them on a table in front of a lighted candle until it is burned through.

- Alternatively, light the candle and burn a leaf or two in the flame, stating your purpose for the herb, whether to protect a home or for healing.

- You can also make a simple infusion of herbs in boiling water to create a herbal liquid to sprinkle around rooms, artefacts or photographs of people, animals or places for power or protection (see below for how to prepare an infusion).

- You can wash floors to be used for ceremonies with the infusion added to a bucket of warm water.

Making an Infusion

- Small quantities of infusion can be prepared by placing one teaspoon of dried herbs or three teaspoons of fresh herbs in a cup and pouring on boiling water.

- For larger amounts use in proportion 30g (1oz) of the plant substance to 600ml (1¼ pints) of water.

- Stir the infusion, chanting to empower the herbs.

- Let the solution stand for five to ten minutes, stirring occasionally.

- After this time has elapsed, strain the infusion and use.

- For a fast infusion at work use a herbal tea bag.

Making a Decoction

- A decoction is a method of extracting healing and magical agents from roots and/or barks.

- The roots and/or bark should be powdered, crushed in a pestle or finely chopped, and 30g (1oz) should be added to 500ml (1 pint) of cold water. Some decoctions are better if left to stand overnight before brewing.

- The mixture should then be simmered until the amount of water is reduced by half.

- Strain before using; squeeze the herbs to get all the liquid out of them, then discard the herbs as with an infusion.

Herbs to Avoid in Pregnancy

I have included below herbs that you may come across elsewhere, as well as those I have discussed specifically in the book. The prohibitions apply to internal use, baths and massage, and to prolonged inhalation through their smoke.

In pregnancy Avoid aloe vera, angelica, autumn crocus, barberry, basil, caraway, cayenne, cedarwood, clary sage, fennel, feverfew, golden seal, hyssop, juniper, male fern, mandrake, marjoram, myrrh, parsley, pennyroyal, poke root, rosemary, rue, sage, southernwood, tansy, tarragon, thuja, thyme, wintergreen, wormwood and yarrow. Other conditions, such as heart problems, raised blood pressure, diabetes and weak kidneys, make it unwise to use some herbs internally. Check with a herbalist if you intend to use herbs medicinally or handle them for prolonged periods.

About the Herbs

Agrimony (*Agrimonia eupatoria*) Good for psychic protection, it will return negative energies to the sender; medicinally, it relieves digestive disorders, liver and bladder problems, cuts and bruises, and throat problems.
Use flowers, leaves, stem and root.
Available as a herb.

Angelica (*Angelica archangelica*) Brings energy, health and long life; offers protection, especially for children and against attacks on the home, whether physical, psychological or psychic. It is anti-bacterial and anti-fungal and is good for digestive disorders, respiratory and liver problems, influenza, poor circulation and painful menstruation. It is especially helpful for older people.
Use leaves, roots and seeds.
Available as a herb.

Anise/aniseed (*Pimpinellla anisum*) Offers protection against all negative influences, physical and psychic, and against nightmares, fears of attack, and anxiety about ageing and infirmity. Good for calming the nervous system, for easing coughs, chest and digestive disorders, and for persistent colic in small children.
Use seeds, flowers and leaves.
Available as a herb, oil and incense.

Basil (*Ocimum basilicum*) Encourages faithful love and trust in love, attracts abundance of all kinds, and protects against intruders, fear of intruders and attacks of all kinds; also takes away anger and indifference. It eases stress, anxiety and indecision, persistent stomach pains and ulcers, fevers, colds and insomnia, and reduces toxicity in the system.
Use leaves and stem.
Available as a herb, oil and incense.

Bay (*Laurus nobilis* or *Pimenta racemosa*) Offers protection, purification, strength and endurance, and is protective against illness and malice in a sachet; enhances fidelity in permanent relationships; induces prophetic abilities and psychic powers. Bay reduces stress, and eases spleen and liver problems, rheumatism and arthritis; it is good for female fertility. Bay leaves can be slightly narcotic and should be used sparingly.

Use leaves and berries.
Available as a herb, oil and incense.

Bistort, also known as Snakeweed or Dragon's Wort (*Polygonum bistorta*) Herb of fertility; also deters malice in others and increases natural intuitive and divinatory powers (good for overcoming spiritual or psychic blockages). A naturally cleansing herb, good for cuts and wounds that will not heal, throat, mouth and tongue disorders, and gastric disorders.
Use roots and leaves.
Available as a herb.

Chamomile, Roman (*Chamaemelum nobile*) or **Chamomile, German** (*Matricaria recutitao*) The most gentle and soothing of herbs, chamomile is sometimes called the children's herb and so can be used for healing all babies' and children's ills and sorrows; it restores confidence after a period of bad luck. Chamomile is good for enhancing self-love and, like rose and lavender, for healing abuse of all kinds. It can be used in all gentle purification rites and also as a healing herb. It soothes anxiety and stress, relieving insomnia, nightmares, gastritis, hyperactivity in children, eye and throat problems, migraines, colic and stomach troubles, especially in children, and respiratory problems.
Use flowers that are widely available in health and food stores.
Available as a herb, oil and incense.

Dandelion (*Taraxacum officinale*) Brings love and long life; enables the free flow of emotions and the emerging of psychic and intuitive awareness. A physical, emotional and psychic cleanser, it is good for the liver, spleen, gall bladder and kidneys, helping to clear obstructions and detoxify the system; it relieves hypertension and eye problems. It also encourages circulation, is helpful against viruses and prevents the build-up of excess fluid and toxins.
Use roots and leaves.
Available as a herb.

Eyebright (*Euphrasia officinalis*) Known as the herb of truth and so important to the Druidic path; an important cleanser of illusion and less than honest influences; also enhances clear psychic vision and so can remove indecision. Medicinally, it is also a cleanser with anti-inflammatory and astringent properties; good for all physical eye problems, sore throats and sinuses.

Use leaves, flowers and twigs.
Available as a herb.

Fennel (*Foeniculum vulgare*) A herb of courage, energy and strength, and of cleansing; fennel will drive away and keep away all harm from people, places and animals. It increases the metabolic rate, and reduces excess fluid and swellings; it is good for all digestive disorders, including those of the gall bladder and spleen, and especially for persistent problems such as colic in babies. It can also be used for detoxifying and for regenerating the liver.
Use seeds, roots and leaves.
Available as a herb, oil and incense.

Fenugreek (*Trigonella foenumgraecum*) A herb associated with increased prosperity over a period of time, not only in resources but also in health and strength; it is a healer as well as a cleanser, and builds up its potency in a series of rituals. One of the oldest healing herbs in use, fenugreek may have travelled to Britain from Mediterranean regions, perhaps via trade routes. It is good for the digestion, wounds and ulcers, and for all chest complaints.
Use seeds.
Available as a herb.

Feverfew (*Tanacetum parthenium*) A cleansing herb, feverfew protects travellers and all who must go to unfamiliar or hostile environments. Medicinally, it is used to reduce stress and anxiety, to help the blood to flow more freely, and to relieve migraines and arthritis.
Use leaves and flowers.
Available as a herb.

Honeysuckle (*Lonicera periclymenum*) Magically it brings abundance in all things, love, luck and prosperity, and so can be used to cleanse away misfortune and sorrow. Medicinally, it is potent against internal bacterial infections; also antibiotic against throat infections, viruses and inflammation of the internal organs. Discard the berries, which are poisonous.
Use flowers.
Available as a herb and incense.

Juniper (*Juniperus communis*) Juniper is a herb of cleansing, used to purify homes and to protect against accidents, thieves and all

forms of illness; it also increases male potency. Medicinally, juniper is antiseptic and diuretic; it is effective against digestive and gastrointestinal inflammations, arthritis, rheumatism, and respiratory conditions, and calms anxieties and stress.
Use berries and twigs
Available as a herb, oil and incense.

Kelp/Bladderwrack (*Fucus visiculosus*) Valuable for Druidess sea rituals; use for protective amulets and rituals to attract prosperity. Cast it into the waves at tide turn to invoke the powers of the realm of the Sea (*see page 55*). Medicinally, kelp strengthens the efficient functioning of the glands, especially an underactive thyroid gland, relieving general debility, hair loss, rheumatism and rheumatoid arthritis; it is a general improver of health and energy.
Use whole plant.
Available as a herb.

Lavender (*Lavandula*) A healing herb that promotes love, especially self-love and gentleness, happiness, health, and both internal and external harmony; it guards against cruelty and spite, and helps grief, sorrow and guilt. Medicinally, lavender relieves stress and anxiety, depression, insomnia, headaches and migraines; it has antiseptic properties, and may heal wounds and burns, and ease throat and chest conditions, so it is also a very gentle cleansing herb.
Use the leaves and flowers.
Available as a herb, oil and incense.

Marigold (*Calendula officinalis*) Fresh marigolds increase positive energies in a room or building; they are protective especially at night and in domestic matters, and the flower helps with stresses caused by legal problems. It also increases psychic awareness, especially of the fairy realms, as well as personal charisma. Marigold is a natural cleanser, being antiseptic and anti-fungal. Medicinally, it is a good all-purpose healer, and is especially potent for all skin problems, headaches, poor circulation, and throat disorders, as well as for painful or delayed menstruation; it helps to heal wounds and damage to any part of the nervous system.
Use flowers and leaves.
Available as a herb, oil and incense.

Marjoram, Sweet (*Majorana hortensis* or *Origanum marjorana*) Brings protection, love, happiness, health and money. Medicinally,

marjoram is cleansing and anti-viral, relieving stress, depression, and recurring headaches and anxieties, and countering signs and fears of ageing; it improves the circulation in the hands and feet, and prevents illnesses from developing.
Use leaves and flowers.
Available as a herb and oil.

Meadowsweet (*Filipendula ulnaria*) Increases peace within the self, between warring factions and globally; brings lasting love, happiness and psychic awareness, especially about those who have wronged you or have malice in their hearts. It is used for both gentle cleansing and healing; it is good for stomach ulcers and infections, eye problems, depression, fevers, rheumatism, arthritis and viruses, especially those involving respiratory difficulties, and bladder and kidney disorders.
Use whole plant.
Available as a herb.

Mint, Water (*Mentha aquatica*), also **Peppermint** (*Mentha piperita*) A purifying herb, driving away all negativity from objects and places and also keeping away illness; bringing sleep and prophetic dreams, it is a natural protector of travellers and attracts money, health, love and success. Medicinally, peppermint especially prevents travel sickness and all other forms of nausea and sickness. It is good for ulcerative colitis and Crohn's disease. A decongestant and anti-spasmodic, peppermint will help coughs and catarrh and relieve headaches, especially those caused by sinus problems. It is also an energiser.
Use parts of plant that grow above ground.
Available as a herb, oil and incense.

Mugwort (*Artemisia vulgaris*) Water darkened with mugwort is used for scrying, and its aroma also increases psychic and prophetic powers; it drives away danger and increases fertility; helps shapeshifting (*see pages 138–40*); and is protective on journeys of all kinds, especially from predators, human and otherwise. It is good for the liver, all menstrual and menopausal problems, digestive disorders and fevers, and is a traditional herb of fertility.
Use leaves and stem.
Available as a herb.

Nettle (*Urtica dioica*) A very defensive and cleansing plant that needs handling with care to avoid stinging yourself; traditionally used to repel strong attack or danger. Nettles also drive and keep away sickness; medicinally, nettles strengthen the whole body and are especially helpful for people who are anaemic, generally weak or have brittle nails, bones and hair. They are good for eczema and rheumatism, as well as for incontinence in both adults and children. Use aerial parts, leaves and stalk.
Available as a herb.

Parsley (*Petroselinum sativum*, also *Petroselinum crispum*) A purification herb, parsley keeps away all harm, alleviates grief and sorrow, and banishes misfortune. A divinatory herb, parsley is said to encourage fertility, love and passion. Medicinally, it is good for the blood, and relieves anaemia as well as skin problems such as eczema. A natural diuretic and antiseptic, parsley also alleviates menstrual and menopausal symptoms, as it contains natural oestrogen.
Use leaves, roots and seeds.
Available as a herb and oil.

Rose/Rose Otto (*Rosa damascena*), **Rose Absolute** (*Rosa centifolia*) The ultimate gentle healing herb of love and reconciliation, especially good for healing the young, the very old and the vulnerable; rose is naturally restorative both physically and of optimism and self-love. It also attracts love and good fortune, heals abuse and trauma of all kinds, especially from childhood, and increases innate clairvoyance and prophecy. Medicinally, it reduces stress and prevents insomnia, and relieves psychosomatic conditions, eating disorders and other addictions. It is good for heart, skin and eye problems, for chronic coughs, for circulatory problems and for all women's hormonal difficulties. It also fights infections and viruses.
Use flowers and hips.
Available as a herb, oil and incense.

Rosemary (*Rosmarinus officinalis*) An important herb of cleansing, rosemary or elf leaf is a herb of protection, driving away illness, malevolence of all kinds, nightmares, fears and sickness; it is said to stave off old age. Rosemary improves the memory and concentration; it can be used as a herb of purification before ceremonies and in divinatory work. Rosemary has anti-bacterial and anti-fungal properties. It is good for relieving headaches, skin problems such as eczema, migraines and depression, and increases energy and improves mobility.

Use leaves and flowers.

Available as a herb, oil and incense.

Sage (*Salvia officinalis*) A healing herb promising longevity, good health and contentment. Burned before divination or meditation, sage increases psychic awareness and allows glimpses of past and future. It is very protective for the home and family, and also for creatures, places and even nations. Medicinally, it strengthens the lungs and the immune system, helping to build up resistance against colds and speeding recovery in cases of debilitating or chronic conditions. It also eases mental exhaustion and increases the ability to concentrate, lifts depression and soothes anxieties.

Use leaves.

Available as a herb, oil and incense.

St John's Wort (*Hypericum perforatum*) A symbol of invincibility, courage, power, the Sun and fertility, St John's wort is used ritually both for purification and healing. It banishes malevolence, earthly and otherwise, from the home. Medicinally, it is chiefly associated with the relief of depression and anxiety-related conditions; a natural pain reliever and anti-inflammatory, it will also alleviate fibrositis, sciatica and pain from rheumatism.

Use all parts that grow above ground, including flowers.

Available as a herb and also carrier oil, in which essential oils are diluted for use.

Tarragon (*Artemesia dracunculus*) Tarragon is used in rituals and in decisions involving shedding the old, and is excellent in all cleansing rituals. It causes regeneration in any and every aspect of living, and helps the user to focus on new targets. Tarragon has a dual action of mildly stimulating the nervous system to overcome restless exhaustion that can stand in the way of relaxation, while also soothing anxieties so sleep comes easily.

Use leaves.

Available as a herb.

Thyme (*Thymus vulgaris*) Like sage, thyme is used ritually to purify areas to be used in ceremony; it can also be used for psychically cleansing the home and places. A divinatory herb, the fourth of the 'parsley, sage, rosemary and thyme' quartet of magical herbs, it offers glimpses of past and future. It is a natural health-bringer, and improves memory and drives away nightmares and phantoms of the night. Medicinally, thyme is a powerful antiseptic, being especially good for wounds that will not heal, for throat infections, and for coughs and respiratory problems.

Use all parts of herb that grow above ground.

Available as a herb, oil and incense.

Vervain (*Verbena officinalis*) Vervain is a purification herb, used both to sweep clean an area before a ceremony and sprinkled in an infusion to bless those who attend. It protects the home, attracting the blessings of nature spirits and land wights or essences. Medicinally, vervain relieves liver and gall bladder disorders, as it is an anti-inflammatory herb; it strengthens the nervous system, reducing tension and the effects of stress. It also eases depression, especially after illness.

Use leaves and buds.

Available as a herb, oil and incense.

The power of various animals is complementary to the power of herbs in healing. Animal power can be used to protect ourselves and others from harm. The next chapter shows you how.

9

Using the Power of Animals

In the Introduction to this book, I mentioned Pomponius Mela's descriptions of the first century AD of nine virgin priestesses living on the island of Sena in France who could, he said, transform themselves into any form of creature they wished. Myths abound of Druids and Druidesses assuming animal form, and modern Druidesses such as Emma Restall Orr, head of the British Druid Order, use the power of spiritual shapeshifting as a source of great spiritual power.

A Shapeshifting Myth

The ultimate shapeshifting Goddess saga was that of the Crone Goddess Cerridwen, who with her cauldron has become a symbol of healing to modern Druidesses. A boy, Gwion, was guarding the Cauldron of Inspiration and Wisdom for Cerridwen, but spilled three drops of the brew on his fingers and licked them.

What interests me most about the legend is that the confident Gwion decided to outwit the angry Goddess by using his shapeshifting powers, newly acquired by him in his first dose of her magical brew. Gwion became a hare and Cerridwen became a hound and pursued him. He took the form of a fish and she an otter. Gwion turned into a bird, Cerridwen a falcon. Finally, he metamorphosed into a grain of corn, but she became a hen and swallowed him up, so establishing her power as superior shapeshifter.

The sixth-century bard Taliesin, who told the story in one of his poems, claimed that he was the long-living transformed Gwion who, nine months later, was reborn from Cerridwen's womb as Taliesin, Radiant Brow, bard, magician supreme and a semi-deity because his new mother was a Goddess.

The Power of Shapeshifting

So what relevance can shapeshifting have to the modern Druidess, assuming you do not want to swallow up the callow youth sent by the local electrical store, who fails to fix your three-week-old cooker?

Shapeshifting, whereby we can absorb the strengths of our chosen power animal and become a fearless wildcat in a power struggle for survival in the office jungle, can be a very good way of amplifying specific energies which we already possess but perhaps do not use effectively.

Different animals can be appropriate for shapeshifting according to the situation. You will begin to make contact with your personal power animal or bird later in this chapter if you do not already have one. However, you can tap into any spirit creature's aura or psychic energy field in order to avoid detection or aggravation. Once you have started to use this method, the animal does not even have to be present. Lions may be in short supply in the average city street, but you can use your awakening psychic powers to conjure one up – psychically of course.

I have focused on creatures that appear in Celtic myths throughout the ages, because magically these seem to work for a number of Druidesses. You can read more about the old stories on-line or in books; over the centuries they have built up layers of magical associations. For example, blackbirds have come to be linked with joy, protection against fear and the Welsh pagan Goddess Rhiannon, because they sang on the tree at the entrance to her realm, the Celtic Otherworld, and acted as doorkeepers. So sweetly did they sing that none was afraid to enter on death. I often use the blackbird when I have to appear on a television or radio show knowing that the presenter is primed not to listen to what I have to say but merely to ridicule it. On a number of occasions when I have used the cheerful blackbird persona the presenters have cracked and told amazing psychic stories from their own lives.

As a modern Druidess you can tap into animal power and protection from absolutely any creature from anywhere in the world, even a mythical one. If you are, for example, waiting for a taxi late at night in a city centre, surrounded by drunks or football hooligans, you might shapeshift into a dragon, wolf or bear, all Celtic power icons still used in Druidry today. You might prefer a tiger or lion through which to express sufficient 'Don't mess with me' power signals that will even penetrate an alcoholic haze.

What will your aggressors see? A not-very-tall, twenty-first-century woman in a travel-creased suit who wants a stiff drink and her bed? Or a snarling wolf? Even allowing for the strange effects of alcohol we can't be sure, but psychically the vibes should be sufficiently menacing to ensure that the would-be predators will lurch off elsewhere.

Alternatively, you may decide to choose a creature to lower your profile, so that you aren't picked on in a morning meeting at work when you haven't prepared any notes. If you need to become unnoticed choose a silent, quiet creature, a shy deer hiding in the thicket. According to folklore, lots of Celtic Goddesses turned into deer when they wanted an hour or so of peace from running the cosmos.

If you do use your Druidess powers to get you out of a tight corner or for purely personal benefit, you can pay the cosmos back by helping out a fellow creature in distress – for example going to the aid of someone you don't like when they have a problem, or doing something to help threatened or ill-treated animals or a polluted river.

Walking On the Wild Side

Now for the technique. On pages 145–6 I have suggested ways of familiarising yourself with a number of power creatures whose persona you might like temporarily to borrow. For shapeshifting in the everyday world you will work with the aura of a visualised creature. Bird auras are usually blue, grey or silver, while animals that live in the wild tend to have brown or dark green auras. As you work close to nature as a Druidess and spend time observing wildlife, you will gradually begin seeing auras on actual living creatures as though they were external bands of light.

- Choose the power creature you are going to merge with and visualise it directly in front of you, standing quite still. Imagine that the creature is as large as you are.

- Focus on the aura or psychic energy field around the visualised creature.

- Inhale slowly through your nose, drawing the coloured light of the aura of the animal into you, and on the out breath through your mouth, pushing your own separate aura boundaries outwards so that the two auras merge. Your aura will be rainbow coloured with one or two shades predominant, and will extend about an arm's length all around you in a sphere.

- As you continue to draw the animal aura into yours, imagine the feelings of the creature filling you with confidence, fierceness or a desire to stay hidden, and exhale on your out breath any vestiges of your own fear or inappropriate anger.

- As you continue to breathe in you will absorb the unique strengths of the creature and will begin to feel the skin or the feathers enclosing your own skin. On your out breaths begin to send out the signals that drive away predators. Alternatively, if you are seeking to be unnoticed, create the aura of the smallness of a mouse, the peace-exuding radiance of a dove or the quiet courage of the dog that sets limits beyond which none can pass.

- Continue to inhale and exhale more quietly but still rhythmically, looking at the scene from the eyes of your power creature.

- As you move, feel the paws padding beneath you, the mighty strides or the almost imperceptible scurry to safety. Before long you will find that the predators have melted away, or that you have passed the danger point: the meeting has ended; a taxi is drawing up alongside you; the police have arrived and cleared away the drunks; or the train has arrived and the carriage nearest to you has couples or families in it.

- When you are ready, exhale outwards first, pushing away the feathers or the fur and inhaling your own separate boundaries.

- Shake your fingers and feet and step out of your power creature, thanking it for safe passage. Do something positive for either an individual member or the species that you chose as protector, or put out seeds for the wild birds.

Personal Totem or Power Animals

Each of us has more affinity with some creatures than with others, and one species may especially resonate with you. This may be a creature that has fascinated you from childhood or even initially terrified you, because you did not understand the strong pull you felt. It may be a domestic creature or one that lives wild in your area; alternatively it may be an exotic creature you saw in an animal park when you were young and which has appeared periodically in dreams. You may find that some wild birds instinctively come close to you, or that an animal at a sanctuary makes eye contact whenever you visit.

Below I have listed animals from the Celtic world that have come to us through myths and poetry transmitted over the centuries; through visualisation work and meditation, they have become important icons to modern Druidesses of their spiritual Celtic roots. You can, of course, substitute creatures from your own wildlife habitat that have similar characteristics, or ones that you would value in your life.

The following qualities are, to me, those that Druidesses today will find helpful in their spiritual and emotional armoury.

Blackbird   Use the sweetness of the blackbird to bring joy into your world and cast away fear and uncertainty when you enter an unfamiliar situation.

Bear   Use the protection of the bear when you are feeling lost or are under threat, and for developing your skills in herbalism and healing generally.

Boar (Wild)   Use the tenacity of the boar when you need courage, and to persist in a venture that meets with opposition. Also useful for connecting with the sensual delights of the natural world.

Bull   Use the strength of the bull for animus power, for dignity, for understanding on the deepest level the ceremonies you create and for giving up short-term gain for long-term advantage. Bulls have traditionally been considered the embodiment of ultimate male strength and sexuality, but obviously are also good for a woman to express her more instinctual side.

Cow   Use the fertility of the cow for bringing abundance into your life, for the patience to nurture others and the willingness to act as a mother to the environment, and to tidy up after other careless humans.

Crane   Use the quiet authority, long memory and wisdom of the crane to argue your case, to silence uproar at work or in your home, and to work towards long-term spiritual understanding.

Deer   Use the swiftness of the deer and its ability to avoid detection to avoid danger or confrontations that serve no useful purpose, and to make the most of your life, even if you did not choose the path.

Dragon   Use the generative power of the dragon to discover and develop hidden potential within yourself and for increasing your personal magical powers. Save the fire power for occasional effect, when others are being totally unreasonable.

Eagle   Use the vision of the eagle for developing wise female power, and for nobility of purpose, benevolent leadership, and the ability to soar spiritually and connect with cosmic knowledge.

Hawk   Use the power of the hawk for focusing on what you want, for increased clairvoyant powers, for achieving worldly success without compromising your principles, and for expanding your horizons both mentally and spiritually.

Hound/the Dog   Use the boundless energy and unwavering guardianship of the hound when you need physical, emotional or psychic protection, to mark out in your mind and to others your territory and limits, and to keep the loyalty of your friends and partner.

Horse   Use the power of the horse to make yourself a strong woman psychically and mentally, to bring fertility of all kinds into your life, to travel to those places that will bring enlightenment as well as pleasure and to live in harmony with a significant other (if you wish).

Lapwing   Use the altruism of the lapwing, the bird that conceals its nest and, if predators come, soars upwards crying to distract them, to help you to protect those who are vulnerable, for treasuring your private moments and experiences, for keeping necessary secrets and for the ability to rise above the material world.

Otter   Use the versatility of the otter to adapt to difficult circumstances, to develop different facets of your life at the same time, to fit spiritual and material needs in harmony and to learn how to best give service to others.

Owl   Use the wise perspectives of the owl for easing transitions at natural change points, for issues concerning female ageing, for listening to and understanding the warnings of your inner voice, and for becoming a wise woman at any age.

Salmon   Use the love of tradition of the salmon that returns to its place of birth to spawn to acquire understanding of your ancestral roots and your spiritual kin, and for increasing personal divinatory and prophetic powers.

Serpent/Snake   Use the transformation of the snake to shed what is no longer of value in your life, and to connect with the essence of womanhood and your inner goddess or higher wisdom.

Sow   Use the earthy fertility of the sow to connect with nature, to value inner beauty and radiance in others, and for discovering what truly matters to you.

Stag   Use the invincibility of the stag to bring out your animus powers at a time when your opinions or rights are being overridden or ignored, and for learning to accept and not fear your growing magical powers.

Swan   Use the harmony of the swan to discover spiritual inner harmony even when your external world is disharmonious, for discovering your still centre and for hearing clairaudiently the hidden music in the natural world.

Wolf   Use the fierce maternal qualities of the wolf to protect yourself and loved ones from hostility of any kind, to make deep friendships with like-minded women and to demand loyalty from colleagues as well as kin.

Wren (or any small brown bird)   Use the survival power of the wren or any other small brown bird to thrive in a fiercely competitive and sometimes uncaring world on your own terms, to develop your prophetic powers and to value what you are as you are.

Choosing a Power Creature

As mentioned in the Introduction, some Druidesses adopt a bird or animal as their secret magical name whose qualities empower their spiritual work. However, others see the power creature as a separate source of power within whose aura they can move when they need its particular strengths.

Although you may identify most strongly with one creature, there may be others whose qualities you find helpful at different times in your life. You may therefore settle on two or three power creatures that may change at different stages of your life and spiritual evolution. Even if you already work with the strength of one animal, you may find it helpful to begin a page in your journal for each of the creatures that seems relevant or that appears regularly in your life.

You can include photographs taken when you have seen the animals in a natural habitat or in a sanctuary. Collect images and information from books, magazines or the Internet about the natural life and the mythology of your chosen creatures. If you are not certain about your power creature, spend time absorbing information and visiting wildlife habitats until one comes to you in a dream or appears in an unusual context, and so the link is made.

Working with Your Power Animal

Once you have made your choice, you will be surprised by the way your power animal keeps cropping up in your life. You may come across your icon in the wild or in unexpected places, or suddenly see articles about it in books and newspapers, and references to it on television and radio will also seem to increase dramatically.

I have already described a process for shapeshifting on pages 141–2, but for some women this process comes later or may never feel right. Below I have suggested alternative ways of spiritually connecting with your power creature/s.

- Sit quietly in woodland, in moments of reverie before sleep or as you awaken, or in the presence of your creature at a conservation park. If you clear your mind, your consciousness may quite spontaneously begin to merge with that of the creature. It may seem that your breathing changes and as you walk in reality, in sleep or half-sleep, you are your power animal, perhaps even suddenly bounding in a half-waking vision into an Otherworld jungle on the back of the animal. There you may see mythical, archetypal, half-wild deities, the Mistress of the Animals or the Lord of the Hunt, who may pause and offer you strength or wisdom.

- Do not force the connection or consciously visualise these other worlds. As you mature spiritually as a Druidess, so these visions will become more frequent and richer. But they are not of our world and so accept glimpses as a bonus and a blessing. Follow whatever animal you have chosen into the magical spiritual or dream planes only when and as the animal leads, and be prepared for the vision to fade when the time is right.

- You can tune more permanently into the strength of a chosen creature by wearing a small silver amulet of the animal, choosing one as your computer screen saver, or finding a tiny wooden or ceramic statue that you can keep in a special purse.

- You can collect amulets of other creatures, as well as your special icon, so that if, for example, you need the courage of the boar, you can carry that amulet for a day or two or keep it under your pillow as you sleep.

Finding the Right Power Source

Here's an exercise to help you find the right power source.

- Create a pack of cards (*see also pages 26 and 167*) on which you paint or stick images of the different power creatures that interest you. Leave one side blank and laminate the cards if possible.

- When you have a tough decision or challenge to face, shuffle the cards and place them face down in a circle, if possible the evening before the event takes place.

• Move your power hand, the one you write with, slowly over each card in turn, progressing clockwise until one instinctively feels right. In time you will have a flash of the creature just before you turn over the card and this will confirm the connection.

• As you hold the chosen image and breathe gently, you will absorb its strengths.

• You can place the card or a relevant amulet beneath your pillow the night before the event.

• If an animal that is not your power creature regularly appears as you work with the cards, explore its energies in more depth. It may be a subsidiary creature that will empower and protect you in different ways from your main animal.

• Selecting a creature at random with the cards can be especially helpful for children if they are worried about a situation, and in time they may quite spontaneously tell you that they have a special bear or stag who comes to them in dreams and lets them ride on its back.

In the next chapter we will explore further the world of the ancestors and deities who form the psychic building blocks on which we climb or wobble (spiritually) towards the stars.

10

Working with the Wise Ancestors

Neolithic burial chambers and passage graves are often found close to ceremonial places in the pre-Christian world. It is speculated that this may be because the ancestors were considered an important part of ritual and ceremonial. It may be that the family dead and tribal chiefs were regarded as a source of wisdom, since it was reasoned that their spirits had access to otherworldly knowledge.

Ancestors in the past, as in the modern world, probably formed the spiritual building blocks of societies, not only by giving life to those who followed after them, but also by transmitting their cultural heritage through the myths and the laws that they handed down. It is in this sense that as modern Druidesses we can value the archetypal wise Druidesses of the past and our personal ancestral kin.

It is the opinion of some researchers of folk history that ceremonies were held at and in passage graves whose entrances were frequently aligned to the Midwinter Solstice and rebirth. One of the most magnificent of these is at Newgrange, in the Boyne Valley, not far from Dublin in Ireland. It lies on a small hillock that is in folk myth said to represent the Mother. A huge passage grave was originally built here in about 3100 BC.

In this chapter we will work with both our own immediate ancestors and those whose root culture we may share spiritually. We will also examine the role of the Celtic deities and spirit beings in modern Druidry, and their relevance to life in the world today.

Today even more than in Celtic times, we draw on a heritage from many cultures, brought to us through invasion, migration and intermarriage. Even in the height of summer in South Africa, Australia or New Zealand, people may feel across the centuries the deep snows of the frozen north and long to hibernate. If we can connect with our psychic roots, then we can understand and work with our natural rhythms.

Rebirth Ritual

You can use the power of the ancestors to bring about rebirth at any stage in your own life when you need to move from a phase that has ended or from a destructive situation into the light of a new beginning.

In this ritual you are not summoning up spirits. But as you recall the names of your personal ancestors, you are making your connection with the past and with the strengths of all the people who have created your unique gene pool. Some of them may just be shadowy names, but others you may know from old photographs or family legends; they may also be people you have recalled from childhood, or those who have recently passed over whose support and guidance you miss. You can carry out the following ritual at any time when you need to move on from the past. It can be a spiritual rebirth, a new perspective or a physical decision to begin change in the outer world.

The rebirth ceremony is best held on the morning of the Midwinter Solstice, which falls on around 21 December in the northern hemisphere and 21 June in the southern hemisphere. On this date in Druidry and witchcraft, the rebirth of the Sun, after it has reached its lowest point of the year in the sky, is celebrated.

You can also adapt the rebirth ceremony for other transition festivals, for example New Year's Day, the Spring Equinox or the Summer Solstice. It also works well on the first day of a new week or month, before a personal milestone event.

Legend tells how in the inner chamber at Newgrange a priestess would wait in the darkness, pouring water on the spiral marked in the rock that indicated where the Solstice shaft of light would fall. The following ritual is an adaptation of this.

- First, draw a spiral to symbolise the spiral on which the priestess would pour water at the passage grave in Newgrange.

- On your front door, or back or balcony door, whichever captures the morning light, or on a window or an inner wall in a room where the morning Sun falls, etch, paint or stick your spiral shape so it will catch the first rays of the light. Prepare this after sunset on the night before the Midwinter Solstice or your special transition time.

- Make also in advance a small dish of empowered water by adding a pinch of sea salt to spring water (still mineral water) and stirring it three times clockwise with a pointed crystal quartz, saying, 'Bless and protect, empower and bring light.'

- Just before dawn, sprinkle your spiral with three drops of the empowered water, saying, 'Mother Earth give birth, new Sun rise, reborn and blessed be.'

- When the sunlight falls on your spiral, trace the path of light with the forefinger of your power hand (the hand you write with), as you do so naming your wise personal ancestors and any special qualities that they had that may help you in the resolution of your future life path. If you do not know a particular ancestor, allow your unconscious mind to speak, for example, 'Grandma Anne give me your patience, Grandfather George give me the courage to say what I believe, Uncle Jim help me to laugh my way out of the gloom in which I find myself.'

- You may find you are naming ancestors you did not know you possessed, but whom later in research you are able to verify. These are usually significant people who have made themselves known psychically because they feel particular affinity with you or walked similar life paths.

- When the Sun has risen go out into the light and extend your arms to the Sun, welcoming the wise ancestors not in their customary home in the west, but in the risen Sun of the east. Ask that they will walk with you on your journey.

- If possible, contact a living relative to whom you have not spoken for some time; that person may be glad to hear from you and may offer you unexpected strength or support.

Finding Your Ancestors

If you know little of your past, try to research your family roots, initially through record offices, and then through census forms and old parish records, some of which are still to be found in the original churches. You can begin with your parents' marriage certificate, as that will give the name of their parents and a location. If you look up your surname on the Internet you may find that another branch of the family has started the search already. Or there may be a family Bible or an elderly relative who is a repository of stories and faded photographs. There may be old journals of adventures or diaries, and you can visit places, perhaps totally unchanged by time, where the people who live on within your body and soul once worked and walked and loved during their lifetime.

Walking in Their Shoes

We often say, 'If I was in your shoes,' meaning if I were you in your position with your pressures and/or opportunities, 'I would . . .'.

But what would you do if you walked in your mother's or your grandfather's shoes, when they were younger? If you lived their experiences even for a few minutes, and understood their fears, how much more might you understand about why they acted as they did? If you did understand, might you be able to forgive or at least to walk away without blaming yourself or them for omissions and commissions? Such experiences are the essences of Druidry: to join ourselves to our own forest, but to cut free from roots that may tangle or unwittingly choke and bind.

Tracing Your Ancestor's Footsteps

So let us try walking back, thinking at each stage about the literal shoes our ancestors would have worn. There are other methods, but this one is very effective.

- Begin in a place, preferably with trees, to connect to the sacred grove that reminds you of some known family strand of family history.

- Allow the image of an ancestor to form. This may not be the one you anticipated but will be the one who has something to teach you or perhaps something for you to understand. The first ancestor is usually a parent or grandparent who may still be alive or, if dead, with whom you have unfinished business or unresolved feelings.

- Focus first on their shoes, whether sturdy lace-ups, boots or clogs, and feel them as though they were on your own feet, heavy or soft, or perhaps with worn soles that let in the rain or caught on stones or cobbles. Walk a little way in those shoes and see how you feel – happy, worried, tired, in pain.

- Keeping the shoes on, walk beside your ancestor, whose spirit form will not be aware of you as they are in their own time frame, perhaps locked in their childhood world, although you can share their emotions. Usually the shoes come from a time before you were born, so you may see your mother skipping in the playground, or your father or grandfather joining the army. It is invariably a period about which they spoke little, perhaps with good reason.

- When the time is right and you have experienced what may feel like days but in fact is usually only a minute or two, you may see another ancestor waiting, another generation back, not necessarily a blood relation to the first. Again, focus on the shoes and feel yourself in them. Generations back there may have been no shoes (sometimes members of poor families shared a pair of boots). If so, look at the feet. They may be calloused or cut – feel how very differently you would walk in the cold on cobbles without any shoes. During this experience you may go back three or four generations.

- When no one else is waiting for you or you feel the everyday world returning, thank your ancestors and your guide, who is present and protecting you. Sit quietly, allowing the new understanding and compassion to fill you.

- When you feel ready, record your experiences in your journal and perhaps contact a living family member with whom you are estranged. Without mentioning your visions, see if gentle questioning can reveal among the living members you encountered some of the blocks from the past that may have made it hard to trust or express love. Some people never change and can live only by destroying those close to them. But in your new knowledge may come freedom.

- You may decide to find out more about your family history and perhaps classify the information to pass on to future generations, or to a local archive if you have no living relations.

- You could revisit the ancestors at regular intervals and perhaps afterwards actually walk in their shoes on the streets in which they lived or worked. Some of the old factories may be disused or have been converted into luxury flats, but visit also industrial and rural life museums to understand more of your distant ancestors' lives. You may feel them beside you on a reconstructed tramway or in the needle makers' cottage.

- One particular ancestor, not necessarily one with whom you initially felt affinity, may begin to appear regularly to you in dreams, or you may detect their presence when you are worried or unhappy. You might smell lavender, rose water, tobacco or oil from a factory, and know that the two worlds are touching.

Finding Your Root Culture

In spite of all this exploration, you could sense that there is a missing link, and that you feel far more connected with your roots when you are in the tombs of Ancient Egypt or on the mountains of Spain, or looking over an industrial landscape half-way across the world from your home. You cannot explain the link genealogically, and yet the peace or joy you experience may momentarily seem more real that the life to which you return.

Often this experience is linked to a past life, either belonging to an ancestor so far back that the connection could not be proven or, as some believe, in a past world you experienced yourself which had such deep significance that it has remained buried in your consciousness. Caesar reported that Druids believed that the soul passed to another body after death and Taliesin, the Celtic bard whose tradition has become mingled with that of a medieval Taliesin, writes of his conscious recall of many incarnations, human and otherwise.

Here's how to connect with your root culture.

- If you can return to a place where you have a strong sense of coming home, try to stay in a hotel or at a camping ground as close as possible to the spot where the feeling was most evident. Spend time quietly there, not attempting to evoke memories but allowing the sounds, the fragrances and the colours of the present scene to form a kaleidoscope within you that may re-form into momentary patchworks of other times.

- Allow yourself to follow what feel like the right pathways in the area, noting any place where access is blocked but you feel instinctively there is or was a way through.

- Use a pendulum to lead you, pausing where it stops swinging to look up at an archway, a carving or a special tree. If it starts to swing anti-clockwise or ceases to move, retrace your steps and see if there is an alternative route, an area of woodland or even a building that elicits a strong positive response. If possible enter it, or enquire about its history.

- Touch stones, gateways, old signs, fountains and crumbling walls on your route and allow impressions to form.

- When you are tired return to your hotel or stop at a café for refreshments and draw an instinctive sketch map of the route you took, which may or may not be the actual way you walked, or a different version without the modern-day diversions.

- In the evening allow yourself to write a spontaneous story of a journey along the route. You may find a character emerging who may resemble you or with whom you feel kinship.

- Allow sleep to come when it is ready and you may again walk the pathways of the day in your dreams.

- Next morning begins the detective work in the local museum, folklore exhibition and libraries. Look particularly for artefacts that were found near the place, which you can handle, such as old pottery, spice jars and fossils, and again let the images form. Use your instinct to guide you to the right historical period with which you connect psychically. Find out about the people who lived or settled in the area a hundred, five hundred or five thousand years ago, and see which of them have the most meaning.

- Finally, draw together in your mind your closing impressions. These may be the sound of the gulls, the smell of burning leaves, the fish market on the quay, spices on market stalls or bushes of wild rosemary. You may hear words in your mind that clarify your impressions.

- See if you can find any old churches and explore them and their grounds – you may find your feet treading familiar paths, hear singing as you walk in procession, or experience once more awe and a sense of familiarity as you look up at the stories depicted in the stained glass windows or painted statues.

- Before you go home, see if there is a local society that you can join which operates on the Internet or has a newsletter, and which will help you to maintain the connection with the place.

- When you get back, explore Ancient Egypt, Seattle, Greece or Wales, wherever your spiritual home may be, in museums, on the Internet, and through legends and images.

- You may get an increasing sense of déjà vu and if you return, whether six weeks or six months later, you may finally understand the link. Your Druidry will become more meaningful as you relate to your spiritual as well as your biological ancestors in ritual and in moments of quiet contemplation.

In the next chapter we look at the world of the Celtic deities and their relevance to the modern Druidess.

11

Working with the Celtic Deities

You can work as a Druid or Druidess without reference to a single Celtic deity if you wish. Some modern Druids and Druidesses worship a Christian deity, while others focus on the Goddess or on more abstract powers of goodness and light.

If you are an orderly soul this might sound a good option, for the Celtic deities are an untidy bunch, spilling out of numerous sources into a giant waterspout of energy. There were hundreds of local Celtic deities, it would seem, of whom about thirty are mentioned in a number of ancient sources.

The Sources of Deity Knowledge

As for the sources, you might try a Celtic history book that can tell you about at least those deities that were known to the Romans and often incorporated into the worship of a mixture of indigenous and Roman gods. An example is Taranis the Gallic Thunder God, whose wheel-shaped amulets and pendants were popular throughout the Celtic-Roman Empire, which held sway from the first century BC to the fourth century AD. Another example is the fierce Gallic Cernunnos, Horned God of the Forest, whose image on a Roman pillar you can see in the Museum de Cluny in Paris.

If you want to read the myths about the deities and the heroes and heroines who sometimes merged, you could try a source such as the *Book of the Dun Cow*, which dates from about 1100 and is said to be the oldest surviving miscellaneous manuscript in Irish literature. It is so called because the vellum upon which it is written is supposedly taken from the hide of St Ciaran's cow at Clonmacnoise in Ireland. It contains material from the eighth and ninth centuries, but it has been claimed by Celtic enthusiasts that this material was handed down orally from centuries before.

A number of the sources have only come down to us from relatively recent translations. For example, the *Mabinogion* is a collection of old Welsh Celtic myths taken from two earlier books called the *Red Book of Hergest* and the *White Book of Rhydderch*. They were translated into English in 1849 by a lover of Celtic material, Lady Charlotte Guest, who claimed that the original versions dated back to 500 BC.

The legends have not stood still and the outpouring of previously unpublished Celtic oral material continues from Wales, Ireland, Scotland, Cornwall, Brittany and the Isle of Man, still Celtic strongholds.

Folklore still holds on to these deities, who have become gloriously mixed up with Celtic saints. St Nectan, the Cornish saint, whose beautiful glen and waterfall are near Boscastle, bears uncanny resemblance in name and associated myths to Nectan, the Irish Celtic water deity who was married to Boanne, the Mother Goddess after whom the river Boyne is named.

When I was researching Druidry, I heard wonderful tales in an Irish pub of Aine the Sun Goddess, who dressed up in her summer finery and shook out her golden hair so that the crops would be ripe when she led the harvest procession to cut the corn on her special hill in Munster.

Modern Druidesses and Celtic Deities

The question is whether modern women should have anything to do with these Celtic deities. I feel that if we dismiss the Celtic deities as unusable because knowledge of them comes from a mixture of periods and sources, that is rather like throwing out the baby with the bathwater. After all, a number of people have said that the major religions of the world are based on unsubstantiated myths.

What we are connecting to are idealised or archetypal power forms that symbolise qualities within ourselves. The various Celtic deity forms, at their most positive, provide foci for expressing the different faces of the God/Goddess or divinity generally, for personifying the forces of nature – mighty, magnificent and sometimes frightening. What is more, they represent symbols of the sanctity of all creation and the immanence or presence of divinity in every tree, plant and rock.

Finally, if you use them as a focus after reading about some of their stories (I have suggested a number of books for you to read on page 199–200, but there are countless Celtic myth books and on-line resources), you may find you dream creatively of them and that some of them may act as wise psychic guardians, helping you to strive for perfection. You may even find yourself writing a new myth as a story or poem, or telling it to your children and becoming part of the fabulous ongoing mythological web that makes us such wondrous creatures of the universe.

Balancing the Good and Evil in the Deities

There was no sharp division between good and evil in the Celtic world. Wise gods and goddesses had their dark sides and might be deities of battle and death as well as healing and birth.

Anyone who has experienced an earthquake or a whirlwind, suffered from the effects of flood or lightning on their homes, or been out in the open air in torrential rain or a storm, has felt the full power of unbridled nature – and so can understand how the Celts expressed their awe in terms of the deities of nature.

Druidesses may live and act only for the greatest good, but they know that we cannot and should not eradicate our shadow self, the inner storms of anger, desire, resentment against injustice or seemingly blind fate; rather, we should take these powers and, facing the fury of our inner storm, work through the feelings and use them to change or resist with courage adversity or temptation. The Celtic deities are a reflection of our own psyches; bland or self-righteous gods and goddesses deny us the opportunity of expressing our own darker emotions creatively.

I believe that if we take our own doubts and troubles within the circle or grove, we can heal and can resolve them there – we can't consign the bad feelings to a Devil or project our own negativity on those who most closely mirror our own faults.

Cerridwen is Dark Mother of prophecy, so she won't just inspire us to sing about sunny days and baby lambs, or tell us how brilliant we are at poetry. She will help us as we perhaps weave our own myths about the deities, in which we take the part of heroine/hero or wise counsellor, not victim or villain, to work through and confront the issues of mortality, suffering and injustice, and come out triumphant on the other side. The world of the Celts and the Celtic deities was a harsh one. We know this from accounts of the battles and from reconstructing daily life from artefacts found. However, its truths and essential courage and optimism make the Celtic deities fine teachers in our world, where essentially the same questions beset us.

Let us now look at the deities whose essences can guide our Druidic work and inspire our everyday lives.

The World of the Deities

Because of the disparate nature of the Celtic tribes that extended over a number of lands, by far the majority of Celtic deities whose names we know were localised in one region. There are no pantheons, as there were in the ancient Greek and Roman civilisations. We do not have statues or images like those of the Greek and Roman goddesses and gods, who were sculpted in the likenesses of beautiful women and virile males. The Celts were gifted craftspeople, but they did not reproduce images of their deities; indeed the first figurines of animals and people did not appear until the second century BC. It was not until the influence of Romanised statuary during the first century AD that more lifelike deity figures, such as Cernunnos and Taranis, the Gallic God of Thunder, appeared.

Finding Celtic Deities

If you want to find Celtic deities for yourself go out into the countryside and look for their faces in hills, trees or rocks. The powers that the Celtic deities possessed related more closely to the natural world, rather than to abstract qualities such as love or courage. They might be worshipped in a tree or at a spring, but not in an enclosed area with the powers restricted within an imperfect if beautiful representation of Divinity. Sometimes it seems that the Celts did not even name their gods specifically when they invoked them, rather knowing in their hearts to whom they spoke.

On pages 161–6 I have listed various Celtic deity forms that you can, if you wish, use in ritual or as a focus for your grove work. You may find one or two who fit well with your lifestyle, and you can find out more about them. You can also write deity names on cards (*see page 167*) and select at random the deities whose strengths may help at a particular time.

Creating a Deity Focus

As you work with the different energies you may wish to create a deity focus to place on your stone in the centre of your grove, in your workspace or near your bed. Make it of a natural material, so that it creates for you the essence of the deity form and is not a life-like representation. You might use a piece of wood to carve a shape, stick shells or crystals on card or canvas, mould clay into an abstract spiral form resembling birds or bees, create an outline of a figure in sand, or combine feathers, leaves, flowers, a piece of bark and dried grasses in a collage. It may be an abstract picture – perhaps copper wire with flowers attached to it, or what seems to be a branch on which you have marked an eye or a spiral. Whatever you create, it represents your unique relationship with Divinity manifest in nature.

Making Offerings

You may like to find a place in your grove, or by water, a special tree or an old stone, to make offerings to the particular deity energies you are seeking in your life. As these will be personal tributes, you might want to find a private setting where offerings will be undisturbed. Again, these can be very personalised: flowers or herbs you have grown and dried; a crystal of which you are fond; a poem or private message you can write and then burn in a candle flame; or a special incense. Or you can make tiny honey cakes and pour a little mead or wine on the ground. You can make a special offerings altar in a secluded place from slate or stone, or just leave your offerings on the earth.

You might, as the Romano-Celts did, offer tokens of your trade – nails, a charm in the shape of a wheel, a silver pen, or a tiny featureless doll filled with lavender or rose to bring blessings on those you love. Or you could leave a rose for reconciliation, or ears of corn or a painted egg for fertility.

As you make each offering, you can enter into a private dialogue, making promises to your inner deity that are even more important to keep than if made to an external God form, asking for blessings.

The Deities of the Celtic World

The following deities have passed into the modern Druidic tradition. You can work with their names and qualities, and go into the kind of country with which they were associated, or visualise them sitting on a rock or in a deep green glen.

Aengus/Oengus Og God of the Dawn, Lord of the Land of Youth. Invoke him for creating or restoring harmony with others, especially in love relationships, and for new beginnings where it is necessary to give up a comfortable but spiritually or emotionally unfulfilling phase or way of life.

Aine Irish Sun and Moon Goddess and Lady of the Harvest. Invoke her for fertility in all its aspects, for receiving reward or credit for work you have done, for developing healing powers, and for getting in tune with the rhythms of your body and with the cycles of the natural world.

Ana/Anu (sometimes linked with **Dana** or **Danu**) A Welsh and Breton Mother Goddess, Mother Earth, also a Moon Goddess and mother of the rivers and streams. Invoke her for all mothering and nurturing issues, for grandmother and grandchildren bonding, for bringing abundance, especially to barren places, and for enhancing your spiritual wisdom, particularly if you are young.

Arduinna Gallic Goddess of the Forest and Patroness of Wild Boar. Invoke her for all matters of female power, especially in the workplace, for clear focus and concentration, and for the courage to stand up for your convictions.

Arianrhod Welsh Goddess of the Full Moon, Time and Destiny. Invoke her for all mystical purposes, for spiritual work under the stars, for the restoration of health and strength after illness or depression, and for taking control of your own destiny.

Badhbh/Nemhain One of the three Irish Crone sisters of battle, likened to a raven or wolf. Invoke her when you must go into battle at work or to preserve your way of life, for matters of fate when life is unfair but you know you cannot change a situation, for comfort in loss, and in divination, that you may see and speak wisely if you are counselling others.

Bel, Belenus, Beli, Belinus, Belenos, Bile The Welsh and Gallic Father God called the Shining; also a god of the corn and barley. Invoke him to give you the authority to overcome prejudice by words or wise actions, for harmonising with the different seasons of the year and the ebbs and flows of your life, and in all fire rituals.

Belisama/Belili The Gallic Goddess of Light and Fire and a Mother Goddess figure. Invoke her for private and group Druidess rituals, especially those involving fire, for learning new crafts and arts, and for illumination spiritually if you seem to be struggling.

Blodeuwedd, Blodwin, Blancheflor The Welsh maiden Lunar Goddess, created from flowers, Goddess of the early summer and blossoming Earth. Invoke her for welcoming summer into your life, spiritually and emotionally, for communicating with the spiritual essences of flowers and for rituals by moonlight.

Boann/Boanne An Irish Mother Goddess and deity of flowing waters and of the Earth they fertilise. Invoke her for all water rituals, for slowing down time if you are overwhelmed, for fertility, and for becoming a guardian of the Earth and fighting against all forms of pollution.

Bran the Blessed An Ancient British Sun God whose symbol was the raven, famed for his prophetic protective powers. Invoke him for courage, for nobility and altruism, for protecting the vulnerable and for using prophetic gifts wisely.

Branwen A beautiful Welsh Cauldron Goddess who suffered

patiently great wrongs at the hands of the cruel Irish king Mathowch. Invoke Branwen for faith in yourself, for resisting emotional blackmail, for justice for women who have been physically or mentally abused, and for keeping your integrity under pressure at work.

Brighid One of the most popular Druidess icons, one of three linked sister Goddesses and, like the Celtic saint Bridget who shares her name, Irish Patroness of Fire and the Sun, smithcraft, the family heart, healing and inspiration. Invoke her in all Sun and fire rituals, for early spring rites, for matters concerning mothers and children, for healing and for inspiration, and as Patroness and wise teacher in modern Druidry, especially of new Druidesses.

Cailleach A generic name for a number of Irish and Scottish Crone Goddesses of winter. Invoke her for winter rituals, for protection of animals, for assisting older women with issues of ageing and for gaining wisdom at any age.

Cernunnos/Herne the Hunter A Gallic Horned God, one form of a number of Celtic Horned Gods, including Herne the Hunter in Ancient Britain (England) and parts of Gaul. Invoke him for increasing animus power, for winter rites and forest ceremonies, for surviving major crises and for pleasure in sexuality.

Cerridwen This Welsh Moon Crone Goddess was keeper of the cauldron of inspiration. Invoke her for personal initiation rites into becoming a Druidess, for protecting Druidesses, for prophecy, to seek poetic inspiration and for herbcraft.

Cliodhna of the Golden Hair Irish Goddess of Healing, the Sea and Beauty. Invoke her in healing and sea rituals, for increasing personal inner beauty and radiance and for valuing it in others over external, media-induced ideals of attractiveness in women, for increasing self-esteem and for reconciliation in relationships.

Coventina A British Goddess of Sacred Springs and Healing Wells, whose name may have been Romanised. Invoke her for safe childbirth, for healing especially of women, for predictive and past-life dreams, and for the flow of love and happiness into your life.

The Dagda A Father God of Ireland, owner of a healing cauldron and a God of Death and Rebirth. Invoke him for animus power, for restoration of hope and trust after a loss, betrayal or setback, for overcoming male prejudice or chauvinism in the workplace, and for protection.

Danu The Irish Mother Goddess and mother of the Irish deities, a shadowy River Goddess rarely described as a person but more as a creative energy. Invoke her for creativity and originality, for the increased flow of the life force when you are feeling dispirited, and for wise use of material resources and time.

Donn The Irish and Welsh God of the Wayside and Travellers, in whose house the dead were believed to rest on the roads to the Afterlife. Invoke him for rest when you are exhausted but are unable to relax, for dream journeys, for safety while travelling and for easing transitions in your life.

Druantia The Fir Tree Goddess, deity of fire, and protectress of mothers and newborn children. Invoke her in purification rituals, for protection especially of the very young, pregnant women and new mothers, to increase your divinatory powers and for all work with trees.

Epona The Horse Goddess of the Gauls and Ancient Britons who was adopted by the Romans. Invoke her for all matters of fertility and motherhood, for travel and trade, to protect horses and horse riders, and for connecting with energies of the land.

Eriu The Irish Sun and Mother Goddess and protectress of the land and all who live in it. Invoke her for matters of trust at work and between lovers, when undertaking new responsibilities, for increasing happiness and optimism, and in rituals to connect with Earth energies.

Grainne An Irish Solar Crone Goddess who, in myth, woke the fertility of the Earth every spring. Invoke her for female power, for fertility, for older women who are enjoying a new relationship or second career, and in harvest rituals of all kinds to reap the fruits of earlier work or endeavour.

The Green Man Ancient British deity of vegetation, trees and green growing things of Earth, and God of the Woodlands. Often seen carved in churches not far from a well, surrounded by foliage. The Green Man, known also as the Hidden One and the Wild

Herdsman, is the archetypal spirit of all vegetation and plants including trees, vegetables, fruits and greenery, predating formal religion and even perhaps the Horned God, consort of the Mother Goddess, with whom he has close associations. Invoke him for fertility rituals, in rituals for the replanting of forests and the restoration of beauty in wasteland, for good harvests in land where there is famine, for early summer rituals and in forest rites.

Gwydion The Welsh master magician deity, sometimes called in folklore the God's Druid, deity of bards and of music and the arts. Invoke him for magical insights, for increasing your creative flow as a Druidess in devising personal rituals, and for ingenuity, especially at times when conventional means or avenues have failed.

Llew The Welsh and Gallic God of Light, who is associated with the mythical annual rebirth of the Sun on the shortest day or Midwinter Solstice on 21 December. Invoke him for all solar rituals, for facing challenges and turning them into opportunity, and for new beginnings after a dark time.

Lugh The Irish God of Light and the Sun. Invoke him in rituals to bring in new ideas or ways of life into practice, for accepting what cannot be changed, knowing that better times will come, to bring peace to war-torn lands and also for altruism.

Mabon The Welsh Divine Child and Inner Child of the Druidess. Invoke him for life-cycle rituals, for merging the innocence and psychic visions of childhood with the mature wisdom acquired as a Druidess, for fulfilling discarded dreams and for breaking out of emotional prisons.

Macha/Nass Another of the Irish Crone Goddess sisters, she is mother of the fertilised Earth and a deity of death leading to rebirth. Invoke her for female intellectual and spiritual power, for resistance against injustice or abuse of any kind, and for closing doors that should have been closed a long time ago and walking with hope into the future.

Mannanan or Mananann mac Lir Manx and Irish God of the Lands of the Blest, a deity of justice and a master magician. Invoke him for sea rituals, for shapeshifting, for walking in two worlds, the magical and the mundane, and for learning to trust one's own judgement.

Modron The Welsh Mother Goddess and a mother of the harvest, of a gentle death and of healing waters. Invoke her for fertility, for water magic, for leaving behind difficult and destructive influences and situations, for loving oneself, and for transforming unhappy experiences into positive knowledge of self and others.

Morgan le Fey/Morgana Welsh and Breton Goddess of the Sea, Death and Winter. Invoke her for female rites of all kinds, for guiding those who must follow a difficult path through life, for acceptance of winter and emotional dark times, for helping older women and for sea rituals.

Nemetona Gallic and British Goddess of the Sacred Groves, warrior Guardian of sacred places and forests (adopted by the Romans). Invoke her for focused power, for all your sacred grove work, for defending what matters to you spiritually, and for integrating male and female energies within relationships to resolve conflict.

Rhiannon Welsh Goddess of the Moon and the Otherworld. Invoke her for meaningful dreams, for Moon magic, for recovering from emotional and physical abuse, and for patience through injustice and intolerance that cannot be overcome because the odds are too great against you.

Taranis The Thunder God of Gaul, whose symbol was the wheel and who was adopted by the Romans. Invoke him for making dramatic changes in your life, for controlled anger when you must fight against injustice, for removing stagnation from your life, and for working with the cycles of the seasons and your life.

Choosing Your Deities

Here's how to choose the appropriate deities to help you in your work.

- Allow images to build up in your mind and perhaps channelled words of wisdom that you hear internally. Note these in your journal and you may find that by working with three or four deities, collecting information but also allowing them to speak to you when you are in the open air, even in a city park or wildlife garden, you can call upon their strengths when you need them in your life.

- You might find it helpful to create or draw symbols for the deities that are important to you; for example, choose a tiny silver bow for Arduinna, Gallic Goddess of the Forest, if you need to act as a huntress in a fierce workday world.

- It may be helpful to write the names and perhaps symbols of those deities who seem relevant to your life as a modern woman on separate, plain white cards, of a size slightly larger than a Tarot card. You may be inspired to paint the images of your favourites on each card and in this way you can create a beautiful, personalised spiritual tool. Even women who are not gifted artists have created beautiful abstract cards. If you wish, write a key word for summoning the strength of each deity on the cards. Laminate the cards and leave one side blank.

- When you have a decision to make or need a spiritual lift, place your cards in a circle face down and, as you did with your animal cards (*see* Chapter 9), pick one with your power hand (the one you write with) by instinct. On occasions I have used the animal and deity cards together, and found that I invariably choose related images, for example Rhiannon and then the blackbird – Rhiannon's bird on occasions where being cheerful, and whistling and singing through adversity, really is the only sensible if unwelcome option.

In the next chapter we will walk or dance the Seasonal Wheel, making the final, essential connection between personal and cosmic ritual.

12

The Druidic Year

Women are very attuned to the seasons and to the prevailing energies. We have all kicked off our shoes at the end of winter and run across the damp grass in the early sunshine, excited by the call of the birds and the indefinable excitement shimmering in the air. We experience sadness while walking home from the shops in early December, even with our bags full of Christmas decorations and festive foods, for it feels as if the year is dying.

Formal orders of Druids and Druidesses, small groups and individual Druidesses mark particular change points of the year with ceremonies that mainly come from the eighteenth century.

We know from early Christian accounts that Christian festivals were grafted on to older pagan festivals and, as the priesthood, Druids would most likely have led celebrations at certain points in the year, such as the coming of spring and the harvest, which would have had agricultural significance to a population whose livelihood was almost entirely linked to the success of the crops and the fertility of the herds. Formal ritual was a universally recognised way of acknowledging that whatever human endeavour and effort was expended, the fertility of the herds, the growth of the crops and the health of the people were – as they are still – subject to forces beyond human control.

Although today modern women may no longer celebrate the annual rebirth of the Sun, natural forces are still in operation outside the sealed, air-conditioned boxes in which many of us live and work. Suddenly the forces make their presence felt and our human-regulated world temporarily grinds to a halt.

I remember staying in a hotel in Los Angeles when an earthquake struck in 1994. Suddenly, civilised, sophisticated America was overthrown by primeval forces. Fortunately, our hotel withstood the shaking and we all took refuge in the darkened coffee shop. Most of us were thankful to be alive, but one man was totally unable to comprehend that he could not have a cooked breakfast and that room service had been suspended. Other people were complaining to the hotel receptionists about the loss of power and the broken glass in their rooms, desperately trying to find someone to put it all right so it could be business as usual. On one of the boulevards a bagel stall opened as usual in spite of a crater in the road.

In modern, affluent society, food is sold packaged or ready cooked, and organic or naturally treated food is a luxury. The process is so remote from the rearing of the animals in conditions that are almost certainly far more inhumane than those practised by the Celts, whose animals shared the living areas of humans. We eat genetically modified vegetables that look shiny and brightly coloured, and have no signs of decay or discoloration. Yet few of us have any real idea of or concern about the toxicity of the chemicals needed to wipe out any imperfections.

Overhead power lines ensure that we have heat and light twenty-four hours a day, every day. Yet there are fears that the electromagnetic fields from these pylons may adversely affect the health of animals grazing beneath and the children who live nearby.

We are cut off from the seasons because until a flood comes, or storms rip down power lines or an earthquake strikes, night can be day, at the flick of a switch, or winter can be summer. We can even holiday under huge, heated glass domes.

Going Back to the Old Ways

But the Wheel of the Year is still turning. The crops ripen and the leaves change colour. A sudden shower of rain, the brilliant radiance of early spring sunshine or carpets of flowers in the parks find echoes within our own inner life cycle and may explain fluctuations in our energy patterns from one week to the next. Seasonally affective disorder (SAD) may not be purely physiological, but may reflect the fact that when it is cold and dark we push on regardless of our bodily and spiritual needs for rest and withdrawal. Even if we no longer feel that we need to make offerings and prayers to the powers of nature for gentle weather and a good harvest, we may still need to recognise the inner seasonal clock, the times when we need to let matters lie fallow or to reap what we have sown. So the Druidic year can be celebrated at a personal symbolic level.

Even if you live in a town, you can become aware of the import-ance of the herds and the crops. As you walk or dance through the year, adapting some of the magical rites practised by modern Druidesses and Druids (and by witches), you are thereby accepting your role as caretaker over what you control, and making offerings and prayers for blessings for those powers that are and will always be beyond human power.

My Personal Journey on the Cosmic Carousel

Let me describe to you a very magical seasonal celebration I attended with my sixteen-year-old daughter Miranda, held by the order of Bards, Ovates and Druids at Avebury Stones in Wiltshire. I had previously preferred to celebrate the passing of the year with private or family-centred rituals. But when I attended the organised ceremony I recognised not only the collective energies that can be created, but also the concept that by celebrating the seasonal change points we are somehow, on a psychic level, accepting our place and function in helping that symbolic wheel to turn. Although next day I was back shopping, working, ferrying the family and fretting over finances, I had been touched on a very deep level.

It was the day before the actual Winter Solstice. The procession of lanterns snaked its way under darkening skies to the stone circle. The beat of the drum and the skirl of the Celtic pipe broke the silence as white-robed Druids and Druidesses, dressed in the green and white of the season, linked hands and created a circle of all present.

Most people were wrapped up warmly against the freezing temperatures. Some of them had come from many miles away; some had joined the procession from the village on impulse, attracted by the dancing lights illuminating the icy blackness.

In the centre were the Druidesses representing the ancient Mothers, clothed in black – the Fates who oversee the time of darkness. An older Druidess representing the old hag of winter was there, too, breaking the ice with her holly staff, challenging us to walk with her into the darkness.

Then all lights were extinguished, and in blackness and silence there was only the muffled prayer of a young Druid that the Sun would be reborn, that light and hope and life would not be snuffed out.

A single light glimmered falteringly as the Druid standing for the Sun King was restored. From that single central flame every lantern was relit.

Then the Druidess, speaking as his mother, rejoiced that her son was reborn, not in a palace, but among the freezing stones to the calling of the distant sheep and cattle. From the circle reaching from earth to sky and back again the eerie call of 'Awen' rose from every mouth, the word calling forth light, life, inspiration, which rose ever louder and higher to the skies.

The Three Mothers had done their work as midwives once more and left the circle; I felt that in some strange way we who were gathered there had played our part and the Wheel of the Year continued to turn.

For me, the most moving part of the ceremony had been when a solemn horn blown deep into the Earth welcomed the ancestors into the circle. I looked at my daughter huddled in my cloak and saw my late mother standing beside us, and even more shadowy in my mind's vision my children's children waiting in this world beyond the world and yet fully within it. Suddenly I understood what it is to be part of a chain of history, and that the importance for me of being a Druidess is that I am taking responsibility for my own small piece of the Earth and those with whom I live or meet in my working life, my personal tribe and community.

The Wheel of the Year

The dates of the solar festivals – the solstices and equinoxes – vary slightly every year because the Earth's orbit around the Sun does not align itself exactly to our calendars. But any diary or ephemeris will give you the correct date.

Some groups of Druidesses and Druids hold their festivals on the weekend nearest to the equinox or solstice because it is easier for people to come together then. For the four intervening lunar festivals, either use the calendar date or begin the evening before. Again, you can use the weekend closest to each of the festival dates.

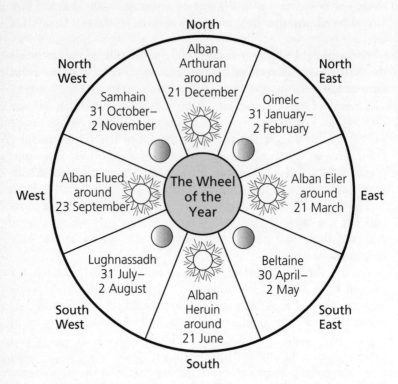

The Wheel of the Year, showing Sun and Moon festivals.

In modern Druidry, although not among the Celts, the four solar festivals are called Alban, meaning the light. This name is said to reflect both the actual and the spiritual light entering the world and the festival. Not every Druid organisation gives the same weight to the four lunar festivals. But we do know that a great deal of ancient folklore does exist around the fire festivals and that they were, as I said earlier, important agriculturally. At some indefinable point, but certainly by the late eighteenth century, the dark half of the year and the Celtic New Year were celebrated at Samhain (Halloween) and the light half of the year, the summer at Beltaine (May Day) and so these also form gateways for new energies.

In modern Druidry and witchcraft three days beginning with the sunset preceding the main festival day are marked as the festival time, so you can if you wish use these days for related activities either alone or with family and friends. I have used them for the equinoxes and solstices as well. Each period of six weeks represents a particular form of power, but you will find that a week before the actual transition you may pick up the energies of the incoming period, even several office floors high in a sea of concrete towers.

Samhain

From sunset on 31 October to sunset 2 November, the time of the Wise Ancestors, looking both backwards to the past and into the future.

Animal Raven.

Tree Apple.

Herbs and incense of Samhain Cypress, dittany, ferns, nutmeg, sage and pine.

Candle colour Orange.

Crystals Deep blue sodalite, dark purple amethyst, grey smoky quartz, deep brown jasper, black jet and obsidian (apache tears).

Symbols As a focus use apples, which are a symbol of health and feature in Halloween love divination, a custom dating from Druidic times; pumpkins, nuts and autumn leaves, mingled with evergreens, as a promise that life continues.

Samhain rituals are potent for protection and overcoming fears, for laying old ghosts in our minds, psychological as well as psychic, for welcoming the positive influence of the family, past and present, and for marking the natural transition between one stage of life and the next.

Personal Activities

- Light huge orange candles and place them in a safe place facing a window to protect your home and light the way home spiritually for those you love who may be far away. Burn the candles from dusk until midnight on Halloween.

- Place a clove of garlic on a west-facing window, saying, 'May only good enter here.' Leave the favourite foods, flowers and photographs of deceased family members at the family hearth or a focal place in the home. Cook great-grandmother's favourite recipes and retell the family legends, especially to younger members of the family.

- Create eight holes instead of a face around a pumpkin and place a candle inside. Peer through each hole to see into other dimensions and receive wisdom.

- Gaze into a fire or candle, and allow images of past worlds and maybe past lives to emerge spontaneously.

Alban Arthuran (the Light of Arthur)

This is the Midwinter Solstice, from sunset for three days around 21 December, according to the astronomical calendar. The rebirth of light and hope; resolving and leaving behind old issues.

Animal Bull.

Tree Holly.

Herbs and incense Bay, cedar, feverfew, holly, juniper, pine and rosemary.

Candle colours White, scarlet and gold.

Crystals Deep green stones such as aventurine, bloodstone or amazonite.

Symbols Use evergreen boughs, especially pine or fir, a circle of alternate red and gold or white candles, small logs of wood, particularly oak and ash found naturally, as a focus for faith that tomorrow is another day, and for inner vision.

Midwinter Solstice rituals are for removing unwanted influences and redundant phases, for home and long-term money plans, for older members of the family, and for the promise of better times ahead if we can just hold on through the rest of the winter either actually, or at a difficult time in our lives. The nights are imperceptibly getting lighter.

Personal Activities

• As the solstice night draws in, light a dark candle and in it burn threads or herbs to represent all you need to leave behind; at sunset light a gold candle from it, using a taper, and then extinguish the dark candle. If you are working with friends or family, they can in turn light their candles from the solstice candle, making wishes for the future.

• Leave the Christmas shopping, and on the day of the solstice go out into the countryside or a local urban woodland and gather evergreen boughs with friends and family; find or buy sprigs of holly, ivy and mistletoe to represent the potential of new life. Make this also the occasion you put up and decorate your solstice/Christmas tree. As you do so sing some of the old songs with pagan overtones, such as *The Holly and the Ivy*, the *Cherry Tree Carol* and *Green Grow the Rushes*.

• As darkness falls create a small fire outdoors or in a tiny metal pot, and burn sprigs of yew, oak and holly, as well as pine needles and rosemary. In this way you are showing your faith that the Sun will shine again – and ritually assisting it to regain power. As you toss on each fragrant handful, name someone who cannot be with you and those causes dear to your heart that will benefit from the renewed power of the Sun.

• On solstice night, fill a metal bowl with water and either alone or with friends or family, in the age-old tradition take it in turns to drip wax from the Christmas candles on to the surface of the water. You will gain an image, as the liquid wax falls on the surface and a second, more permanent image as the wax sets. The first will indicate an area that will bear fruit over the coming days, and the second ways in which you can maximise the energies of the ascending light. Wash out the bowl between readings.

• From clay create your own santons. These are tiny, nativity-type figures that originate in France, and include miniature statues of

local characters and family members. The scene can be adapted
to the rebirth of the Sun/Goddess myths; paint them and set
them around your tree or in a cave made from rocks and crystals.

Imbolc/Oimelc

Imbolc (in the belly of the Mother) or Oimelc (the feast of ewes'
milk) from sunset on 31 January to sunset on 2 February. The
rising of the light and the stirring of new hope.

Animal Serpent.

Tree Willow.

Incenses and herbs Angelica, basil, benzoin, celandine, heather
and myrrh.

Candle colours Pale pink, green, blue and white.

Crystals Dark red gemstones such as garnet, but also purple
amethyst, pink rose quartz and gentle white moonstone for fertility
and awakening feelings.

Symbols Use the very first snowdrops or very early budding leaves,
or flowers, milk, seeds and honey.

Imbolc rituals will give healing and spiritual nourishment in the
form of spiritual milk; some modern Druidesses will find them
useful for the awakening of love and trust, whether at the festival
time or after a period of betrayal or emotional loss.

Personal Activities

- In age-old tradition, pour fresh milk on to the Earth as a tribute
  to the Mother and, as you do so, ask for fertility in any aspect of
  your life for which you need it.

- On the night of 1 February, place night lights safely at every
  window to welcome Brighid (Irish patroness of Fire and the Sun)
  into your home.

- Make a tiny straw bed and in it place a small doll dressed in
  white, with a quartz crystal on the heart to represent the maiden
  Brighid. Pour a little honey on the bed and three drops of milk;
  surround it with the first greenery or buds of spring. Place in the
  straw symbols of the blessings you would like in your life,

whether tiny charms related to your craft or something connected with your home.

- Take a ceramic, heat-proof bowl of milk and in it drop ice-cubes to represent the cold of winter; gently melt the ice with a small candle or burner beneath the bowl, stirring it and naming the energies you wish to move in or through your life to awaken your personal spring.

- Create a circle of pink or blue candles and sit within it, absorbing the light of the new season.

Alban Eiler

The Light of the Earth or Vernal Equinox from sunset for three days around 21 March, according to the astronomical calendar. The triumph of the light; planting the seeds of new ventures.

Animal Hare.

Tree Birch.

Herbs and incenses Celandine, cinquefoil, crocus, daffodil, honeysuckle, primrose, sage, tansy, thyme and violets.

Candle colours Yellow and bright green.

Crystals Sparkling yellow crystals, such as citrine, the strengthening stone, yellow beryl, the energiser, or a yellow rutilated quartz with streaks of gold, the regenerator, for your spring talisman.

Symbols Use eggs, any spring flowers or leaves in bud, a sprouting pot of seeds, pottery or china rabbits, birds or feathers as a focus for your own spiralling energies.

Spring Equinox rituals will bring new hopes, new beginnings, new relationships and life changes. They are good for anything to do with fertility, pregnancy, babies, children, new-flowering love, spiritual as well as actual spring cleaning, exploration actual and spiritual, and incubating new projects and plans to be fulfilled later in the year.

Personal Activities

- Paint eggs using vegetable dye, with flowers, Mother Goddess spirals, birds and bees, and offer them to the Mother on a basket of spring flowers and leaves.

- For increasing fertility, prick an egg and take out all the white and yellow. Pass the shell through a beeswax candle flame or a small fire as the equinox dawns. Then carefully cut it in half and leave the shell halves open for the Sun or light to shine on them.

- On the first night of the New Moon after the Spring Equinox, split the shell and place a tiny moonstone in one half, leaving it on the window ledge until the Full Moon. Place a silver pin in the other half and also leave open to the moonlight.

- On the night of the Full Moon, prick the moonstone very gently with the silver pin and leave pin and moonstone in one half of the egg, so that they touch all night. The next morning close the egg and wrap up egg, pin and moonstone until the Moon leaves the sky. Then you should bury them and repeat the ritual. This can help not only for conceiving babies but also for re-establishing the natural rhythms of your life to bring any new venture to birth.

- Spring clean your psyche. Answer any correspondence that is piling up. Deal with unavoidable issues. Change your routine so that you rise an hour earlier and can enjoy the growing light, perhaps walking to work or sitting in the spring sunshine on your balcony or in your garden. Initiate those projects you always meant to by first clearing out the clutter of old commitments or activities that you no longer enjoy.

- Visit sacred waters or a clear river or pond on equinox morn, and witness the light dancing; cast a tiny crystal in the water and, as it splashes, you will be rewarded by a momentary image framed in light that will help you to plan your future path.

- Make equinox water by leaving it in a clear dish from dawn until noon. Use this for revitalising office plants, trees in urban spaces, or polluted water courses, and for encouraging new growth in places that are no longer beautiful.

- Plant seeds, if necessary under glass, to symbolise hopes for the future, placing tiny equinox crystals or jade in the soil at each corner, and moistening them with your equinox water.

Beltaine or Beltane

For three days from sunset on 30 April to sunset on 2 May, for the uniting of earth and sky and for the unbridled life force.

Animal Cow.

Tree Hawthorn.

Incense and herbs Almond, angelica, ash, cowslip, frankincense, hawthorn, lilac, marigold and roses for love.

Candle colours Dark green, scarlet and silver candles.

Crystals Sparkling citrine, clear crystal quartz, golden tiger's eye, amber and topaz.

Symbols Fresh greenery, morning dew collected on a dropper, flowers.

Beltane rituals are for maximising the fertility energies first experienced at the equinox, whether for conceiving a child or for bringing a business matter to fruition. They can improve health and stimulate an increase in energy, optimism and self-confidence as the light and warmth move into summer.

Personal Activities

• Rise at dawn on May Day morning and wash your face in the morning dew (you can collect it with an eye dropper) for an infusion of the pure life force and for peak potency in any aspect of your life.

• Fill small baskets with garden flowers or greenery and leave them on the doorsteps of anyone who is sick or lonely to spread the abundance of the season.

• Visit a sacred well in accordance with tradition just before sunrise and walk around it three times sunwise (clockwise), drinking the water if possible and asking for healing for yourself or your loved ones; tie a ribbon to a nearby tree.

• Decorate a tree or branches from a tree with flowers, ribbons and bells, and your Maytime symbols. Spiral around them, allowing your feet to trace and amplify the energies of the Earth.

• Make a small fire and burn as many of the sacred woods as you can find that traditionally made up the Beltaine fire. These were willow, hazel, alder, birch, ash, yew, elm, rowan and oak. Alternatively, use woods local to your area. When the fire is burned though, scatter a few of the ashes to the four winds from a hilltop, sending your wishes for the future with them. Bury the rest to bring fertility to waste or barren land.

Alban Heruin, the Light of the Shore

For three days from sunset around 21 June, according to the Astronomical calendar, for power, joy and courage.

Animal Bear.

Tree Oak.

Herbs and incenses Chamomile, elder, fennel, lavender, St John's wort and verbena.

Candle colours Red, orange and gold.

Crystals Brilliant red or orange crystals; stones of the Sun, such as amber, carnelian, orange, beryl or jasper and sunstone; also crystal quartz.

Symbols Use brightly coloured flowers, oak boughs, golden fern pollen, which is said to reveal buried treasure wherever it falls, scarlet, orange and yellow ribbons, gold-coloured coins, suncatchers and golden fruits.

Summer Solstice rituals are good for success, happiness, strength, identity, wealth, fertility, adolescents and young adults, career and travel.

Personal Activities

• On the Summer Solstice, greet the dawn by lighting a lantern just before sunrise, from an east-facing hill or plain. Spend the day in the open air and then say farewell to the Sun on a west-facing slope, lighting your lantern once more to give the Sun power even as it descends.

• Cast golden flowers or herbs into the air from a hill, a handful at a time, making empowerments for courage and achievement to the winds. Where they land and take root represents in the old traditions places of buried treasure or, as here, symbolises new or buried talents you can develop to realise your hidden potential.

• Make your solstice water, the most potent Sun water of the year, leaving water in a gold-coloured dish surrounded by golden-coloured flowers from dusk on the Solstice Eve until noon on the Longest Day. This is especially healing and empowering, and you can keep it in clear glass or gold-coloured bottles to drink or add to bath water to give you energy and confidence.

• Make a small Sun wheel garden, either indoors or outside, using the flowering herbs of midsummer, vervain and St John's wort, Sun herbs such as frankincense, juniper, rosemary and saffron, and all other yellow or golden flowers. Arrange them in the form of a wheel and fill in the centre with tiny, golden crystals or glass nuggets. You can breathe in the golden light from your living Sun wheel.

• Light Sun oils, such as frankincense, juniper, rosemary, orange or benzoin, or burn them as incense to bring the Sun power into your home or workplace.

Lughnassadh

From sunset on 31 July to sunset on 2 August, the first corn harvest, a festival of willing sacrifice, arbitration, contracts and justice.

Animal Stag.

Tree Alder.

Herbs and incense Cedarwood, cinnamon, fenugreek, ginger, heather, myrtle and sunflowers.

Candle colours Golden brown or dark yellow.

Crystals Tiger's eye, fossilised woods, amber, rutilated quartz, or dark yellow and brown stones.

Symbols Use a straw object as your focus, such as a corn dolly, a corn knot or a straw hat, perhaps decorated with poppies or cornflowers, or a container of mixed cereals.

Lughnassadh rituals focus on justice, rights, partnerships, both personal and legal, promotion and career advancement, and the regularising of personal finances. With corn and corn dollies a feature of the time, fertility is also favoured, perhaps preparing for future ventures or getting healthy to become pregnant in the future.

Personal Activities

• Use corn or dried grasses to create corn knots and Corn Mother figures (a featureless head, arms, body and legs) tied with red and blue threads; hang them in the home through the winter to bring protection, and burn them on the first Monday after Twelfth Night or on the Spring Equinox fires.

• If you want to make a Corn King, you can burn him at Lughnassadh; scatter the ashes in your garden or on indoor plants to bring abundance to the home during the winter.

• Make bread with milk on Lughnassadh Eve, a tradition that became associated with the Virgin Mary. As you stir the mix in turn with friends and family, make wishes for abundance and the harvest you wish to reap during the coming months. At dawn crumble the bread to share with friends and family, and leave offerings of crumbs for the wild birds.

• If you feel you have been unjustly treated and cannot put matters right, knot dried grasses, one for each injustice, and cast them on the waters or bury them, planting late-flowering seeds or autumn flowers.

• Arrange journeys to see, or write to and telephone, friends and relations, making plans to meet, as this is a time when tribes get together before the long winter.

Alban Elued

Light on the Water or Autumnal Equinox for three days from sunset around 23 September, a festival of abundance and of balancing gain and loss.

Animal Salmon.

Tree White poplar or hazel.

Herbs and incenses Ferns, geranium, myrrh, pine and Solomon's seal.

Candle colours Blue for the autumn rain and green for the Earth Mother.

Crystals Soft blue crystals, such as blue lace agate, blue beryl or azurite.

Symbols Choose coppery, yellow or orange leaves, willow boughs, harvest fruits such as apples, nuts, root vegetables, and pottery or china geese. Also use as a focus knots of corn, wheat or barley from the earlier harvest, and copper or bronze coins to ensure enough money and happy family relationships.

Autumn Equinox rituals are for mending quarrels, for the fruition of long-term goals, for reaping the benefits of earlier input, for love and relationships, especially concerning the family, adult children, brothers and sisters, for friendships and for issues of material security for the months ahead.

Personal Activities

- Work by the sea at sunset and cast as pebbles into the dying light of the water all regrets, resentments, sorrows, failures and unfinished business from the previous months that you do not wish to carry forward into the winter.

- Take a bowl containing equal numbers of nuts and seeds and work outdoors. Name a success or achievement that has materialised by the Autumn Equinox and eat a nut; then name a failure or loss and cast a seed into the ground. Continue until you have eaten and shed the same number and can think of no more; bury the rest beneath a fruit- or nut-bearing tree.

- Sweep up autumn leaves into a pile; jump up and down in it as you did when you were a child, expressing joy at the promise of the coming days, and naming opportunities and all you can achieve in winter. Finally scatter the leaves and let the good and the bad, the gains and the losses, be carried equally on the wind.

- Prepare a feast of fruits and vegetables, of bread, cider and barley wine, or fruit cup, and warming soups, and hold an equinox party. Make offerings to the land of barley wine, ale, mead and bread, and as you pass around a communal cup, send individual blessings to people and places where there is dearth; hold an auction of hoarded personal treasures and send the money to a charity that relieves famine and poverty.

• Contact anyone from whom you are estranged, sending autumn flowers or a plant you have nurtured, or a basket of produce as a peace offering; if your reconciliatory gestures are rejected, at least you can move forward, knowing you tried. Alternatively, help an organisation concerned with peace.

In the next chapter I suggest ways in which you can develop as a Druidess, and work more formally with others as a Druidess, if you wish to do so.

13

Becoming a Druidess: the Next Stage

There are many ways in which a Druidess can express her spirituality. These range from a love of nature that enriches the everyday world, to training with and working within an established Druid Order (*see list on pages 202–4*), and then perhaps even officiating informally at weddings or naming ceremonies.

As the principles of Druidry become more accessible and less remote from modern living, so informal or folk Druidry will become increasingly important in the lives of women particularly, as a way of connecting with natural energies and using this connection to enrich work and family life. I will probably always remain a relatively solitary Druidess, using Druidry with friends and family as a very personal way of life that has enriched and empowered me, as well as helped me to develop a much more harmonious spiritual centre in my frantic world.

Even if you do not want to join a formal Order, you can find on the Internet details about organisations such as the British Druid Order, which welcomes non-members to public ceremonies; other Orders also allow the family and friends of members, or just interested observers, to join solstice and equinox celebrations even within Stonehenge.

All Druidesses and Druids are concerned with the environment and act as caretakers of the natural world, although there are many degrees of involvement. Some feel, as I do, that teaching future generations by example is the most vital role – and one that can be carried out best by being fully involved in everyday life.

My advice is to go slowly. When you have found out basic information about a number of groups, make contact by writing to them or emailing them, and then go along to a public ceremony. There are no solemn vows to take, no promises of secrecy, no secret passwords, handshakes or signs, and generally no clergy as such in most branches of traditional Druidry. Most Orders will have a chosen chief, an Archdruid or Archdruidess (or often both), to act as a focus; they will be expected to take their turn at the communal showers or with washing up at camps.

There are opportunities to attend camps where Druidesses and Druids, and their families and friends, live together for a few days, sometimes in huge yurts (large, circular tents). You will also find all manner of workshops, lectures and weekends advertised on Druidic sites on the Internet; some will be held in hotels, some in private homes and a number at camps. In addition, some pagan organisations have open meetings and celebrations at ancient sites that you can attend, which will be similar in their focus on a love of the Earth and respect for all her creatures and their habitats.

Different Forms of Druidry

Only you will know which form of Druidry appeals most to you at this time. Many methods are possible, from working on your own to joining a formal group.

Working as a Solitary Practitioner

This is by far the most common and easiest method as you carry your grove with you; using the contents of your crane bag, you can set up a working space anywhere. You can also fit in your Druidry with work and family commitments, and gradually expand your Druidic time and space to develop a rich inner spirituality. One bonus is that you have a very direct contact with nature, with nature spirits and with wise Druidesses of the past.

The drawback – or you may see it as an advantage – is that you do not get input from others. But there are a great number of books that you can read for inspiration and you can, through on-line groves, make contact with other solitary Druids. As a solitary practitioner, it is essential to keep your journal up to date as a record of your work, so that you can read back if you lack inspiration. Remember to keep back-up copies.

As a solitary Druidess your seasonal celebrations can form a personal affirmation of power and connection with the natural world, and can add depth and meaning to modern commercial festivals for family and friends.

Forming Your Own Group

This can be as large or small as you wish, though the Druidic college of nine priestesses that I describe below is a workable number. You will need someone in your group with an organisational flair to arrange the relatively mundane but essential aspects, such as buying candles and so on from a communal fund, deciding where and when to meet, and making sure that the most dreamy Druidess or Druid won't stand at the wrong bus stop on a planned visit to a sacred site. You can rotate between each other's houses and gardens, or find a cheap room to hire in a community centre with a few trees around it for weekly/monthly meetings.

You will also need someone to organise and plan the minutiae of rituals. You can take it in turns to lead rituals, or you may find that different members have different skills, from creating chants to singing to making seasonal decorations. Keep it all very fluid, and divert dominant personalities into specific roles (there's no room for gurus in this gentlest of philosophies). If there are men as well as women in the group, ensure that the women don't do all the candlestick polishing and always arrange the refreshments, while the men get to be cosmic engine driver every time.

You can also plan regular outings to the seashore, to the forest and to sacred stone circles. If you normally carry out your ritual in a town, weekends away can help you to celebrate the festivals close to the Earth. It is entirely up to you whether you camp close to nature, or repair to a motel for meals and hot baths in between your forays into the lakes and woods.

Family participation in a group is debatable. It can be good to invite children and partners to major seasonal celebrations or even for a weekend's camp, but it is important that the spirituality does not get diluted by partners talking about ball games, or by children fighting or complaining that they are bored or cold. Also, if some members of your families don't get on, then peace can be in short supply even among spiritual sisters.

You will need somewhere to keep your equipment. You might store it at different homes, as long as there are standby arrangements if the person storing it cannot turn up on a certain night. You can all shop together for major items, which offers a good excuse for days at craft and antique fairs.

You can of course go along to public ceremonies, still retaining your cohesion, perhaps by holding a short ceremony privately before or afterwards.

A College of Nine Priestesses

If you know eight like-minded women (an age mix is good) this is a very special form of Druidry that can lead to deep spiritual ties. You do not need a leader, just people to organise the different aspects. If a member leaves, because she moves or has changed career or personal circumstances, you can invite someone else to join.

It is up to you how frequently you meet but you may decide to have regular weekly learning/teaching sessions, in which people take it in turns to study and explain their personal interests, whether Celtic myths, ancient history, megaliths or a crash course in Gaelic. Printed notes can be added to individual journals to build up a collective knowledge base.

You can create a communal manual with rituals and information about different aspects of Druidry that is added to regularly by the group scribe, who can also keep the healing section up to date (*see page 86*). You may decide to visit sacred sites, especially with those that have some knowledge of folklore about Druidesses or have Celtic connections.

Some women, whether they are solitary practitioners or belong to formal or informal groups, dedicate themselves to one of the Celtic Goddesses, especially Brighid. But you could choose Cerridwen, Arianrhod or one of the other Goddesses (*see pages 161–6*) for your group focus. Druantia, the Silver Fir Goddess and Mother of the Tree Alphabet, is sometimes chosen by groups who work with divinatory forms.

You can find pictures on the Internet of sites dedicated to your own deities and perhaps create your personal empowerment and dedication to Brighid or Cerridwen with which you begin your ceremonies. If you choose a Moon deity, meet on the Full Moons. For a solar deity, have monthly dawn, noon or sunset ceremonies in her honour.

The college of nine women is a very open form of Druidry and can evolve according to your own needs and concepts of spirituality. For example, if you like St Bridget, or Brighid, and maybe if you listen to the old tales of Ireland, preferably in a hostelry in Kildare in Ireland itself, like the Druidesses dedicated to the Goddess Brighid, have a sacred flame, a small nightlight you burn in each of your homes in turn for twenty-four hours, lighting a larger communal flame for the duration of your meeting.

You may wish to collect permanent treasures (of course you can do this in any group), such as a bronzed fireproof cauldron that you can use for scrying and as a source of fire, a silver chalice for your water, an engraved silver dish for salt and a proper incense censer.

Choosing a Site and Time for Your Special Ceremonies

You will need to deal with the question of where to hold your ceremonies first. Visit sites in your area to find a suitable one, as some ancient monuments are fenced off.

The National Trust owns Avebury but the stones are totally accessible, and there are any number of individual stones on which you could focus a ritual on this huge site. It is a good idea to check with the National Trust first, but a number of formal and informal groups do work there. The stones at Stonehenge, in contrast, are fenced off, and the circle can only be accessed with special permission. English Heritage does not allow ceremonies after dark for safety reasons.

If you live in places where there are no stone circles, there will still be a profusion of indigenous sacred sites, close to which you can hold ceremonies. In some parts of the world, especially in North America, open-air labyrinths are being created and there are some beautiful huge turf ones with free access in the United States and Canada that are perfect for a group of Druidesses to use. Enter the words *labyrinth* and *turf* on your Web browser and suggestions will appear in a number of States.

I would not suggest advertising an open meeting unless you have an organised large group, because all who come along may not be interested in Druidry. At first, if you know someone with a large private garden use that, or get permission to work in an enclosed botanical garden. You can then relax, knowing that you are working with people you trust and that you will not be disturbed. It can be helpful to attend a variety of Druidic public ceremonies before organising your own large gatherings to pick up practical know-how.

You need to set a time and date, making sure that others can easily travel to your location on the day. You might like to make a ceremony the centre of a more extended celebration. For example, you could choose Glastonbury Tor in Somerset, a site that is completely open, at a time when other groups will not be using it, the day before a festival or mid-morning, and arrange accommodation in the town so that you and the group can explore the environs and the other sacred places nearby on your pilgrimage.

If the weather is truly foul and you are working in a wild spot or one that takes some time to reach, you may wish to plan an alternative venue, perhaps a large garage or shed that can be instantly transformed into an indoor grove with branches and a central water feature or rock.

Formal Groups

These can vary from those that you join and then choose how closely to participate in, to ones with organised training courses and regular grove meetings. In the resources section on pages 202–4, I give the addresses of a number of formal Druidic organisations and very brief details of their emphasis.

Take as much care choosing your group as you would if you were involved in any other organisation. If you have started your own group, you may decide to affiliate with a more formal organisation when you have exhausted your own collective input. The groups I have encountered have all been incredibly helpful and welcoming, but trust your own judgement as to what is right for you.

Study the group's website, not only for events and organisation, but also for the additional material it provides – rituals, the interpretation of mythology and its philosophies. Some groups have a strong Celtic emphasis and may suit you if you have a creative approach to the past, but others have evolved from the Revivalist movements. Occasionally women still come across patriarchal organisations. This may suit some men, just as some women like working within a single sex college.

Some groups organise correspondence courses that can be helpful if you live far from a group or have family commitments. The Order of Bards, Ovates and Druids (OBOD) combines the best of both worlds with an excellent tutorial system and as much or as little group contact as you require through organised groves, seed groups run by members, and organised workshops and camps.

Most Druidic courses cost very little. You should expect to pay at the most a few hundred pounds over three years for a full correspondence course, not all of it up front. There are various instalment arrangements and if you cannot afford to pay for a course it is worth asking about bursaries. OBOD sends introductory material free of charge.

Some workshops offered by individual Druids/Druidesses or pagans can seem very expensive, but many do offer meals and accommodation. Be selective and ask what you will be taught and by what methods, whether the weekend is organised by experts in, for example, Celtic mythology and if you will visit local sacred sites with an expert. Other workshops offer mainly experience sharing. Be selective and remember that the most expensive is not always the best.

I have not come across a single-sex female Order, although there are a number of excellent goddess organisations, and the international Fellowship of Isis does have affiliated Druidic orders that are goddess centred.

A Word of Warning

Even in Druidry, there is the very occasional rogue group, demanding secrecy, offering strange initiation rites with a Druid of the opposite sex, and recommending drugs for out-of-body experiences and the like. These people are not genuine Druidesses or Druids. If anything about the initial approach makes you feel uncomfortable, then back off. No one from a genuine organisation will ask you to meet a stranger in a lonely place or club, or ask for really personal details.

Fitting Formal Druidry Into Your Life

A number of organisations have groups in many areas and in different countries. If an organisation works and teaches through groves, find out how often you would be expected to attend, what hours and where you would meet. You may have other commitments, and if you are constantly worrying about babysitters or long journeys, organised spirituality may become a chore. Sometimes waiting a few years and trying a less-demanding avenue, such as lone practice, initially means that you can evolve spiritually in a way that harmonises with rather than puts pressure on you.

The Structure of Formal Druidry

Strabo, a Greek geographer (64 BC–AD 21), writes at the end of the first century BC of three kinds of Druids: the Bards, the Vates and the Druids. 'The Bards are singers and poets; the Vates, diviners and natural philosophers; while the Druids, in addition to natural philosophy, study also moral philosophy.' As a Greek, he disregards the existence of Druidesses – mere women could not possibly hold office or learn anything.

A significant number of modern orders still structure the Druidic course or path in this way, so that you progress through being a Bard to an Ovate and finally a Druidess. Other, less formal organisations, however, consider the divisions as part of an earlier élitism that ran through all aspects of the occult and so was artificial. Certainly, if you are working as a solitary Druidess or as part of an informal group, being a Druidess will involve almost from the beginning the creative inspiration of the bardic aspects, divination and prophecy of the ovate, and finally the Druidic authority as wise counsellor, peacemaker and repository of wisdom and knowledge.

There is considerable overlap of what are essentially three aspects of the same concept. Of course, if you do follow a more formal training, then the longer you study, the more knowledge you will acquire. By perseverance and learning the Druidess is more knowledgeable, if not wiser, than the Bard.

It has been suggested in Classical sources that full Druidic training may have taken nineteen years and I have read accounts of it lasting even longer. All would argue that Druidry is for life, and much of the wisdom you will not acquire from direct teaching, but from your own spiritual explorations of the outer world and your inner self, and above all from direct interactions with nature.

For many Druidesses like myself, who have practised the craft alone for a large part of our lifetimes – long before we even realised we were Druidesses – formal training can be inspirational, but is only a small part of living and working with nature as a means, not of learning to perform Harry Potter-type magic, but of personal spiritual evolution and healing of self and others.

I am also working with the recently formed Druidic College of Healing and increasingly there will be offshoots of existing orders and the pooling of resources with other pagan spiritualities.

The Druidess in the Wider World

As I have said throughout the book, the wiser you become, the more positive influence you can bring to bear on a world in need of wisdom and healing. You will teach primarily by example, by pointing out to the world-weary the wondrous universe outside the office window, beyond the simulated battles of the games console, and by droning on ad nauseam to anyone who will listen, and especially those who shut their ears and drop soft drink cans, about the need to conserve that beauty.

You are the priestess who works quietly and who slips easily between everyday responsibilities and the Otherworld. Behind you in the looking glass you can see the Wise Ancestors who live on in your genes and your soul, and ahead through the mists you can observe the waiting generations for whom you are preparing to make the world a fit place to inherit.

We do not know for sure what happens when we die. When we walk in Druidic ritual towards the east, the direction of rebirth, we may hope that we can take with us as our grave goods the gifts and wise lessons of this life and our essential self, funny, scatty and sometimes ratty, into that rising Sun.

I am increasingly aware of my own mortality. My own mother died in her forties and I am now ten years older than she was when we said goodbye. But I take courage from the singing of the birds, the flowing of the tide, the rustling of the leaves and the light that rises clear and glorious even on this less than summery August day.

Druidry is all about hope and faith, and every small, positive deed and word make the world a better, more joyous place.

I hope this book has been helpful to you, not as an infallible guide to instant and everlasting happiness, but in offering suggestions of ways for a woman to enjoy every moment of sunlight, and to learn to walk the way of wisdom and tranquillity (which I am still practising and stumbling along) to the promise of tomorrow's brilliant dawn.

Appendix – Significant Dates in Druidry

The Origins of Druidry

Given that, like all ancient oral traditions, the origins of Druidry are obscured by the mists of time, a spiritual connection with archetypal Celtic Druidesses can be made by some Druidesses through visiting natural places and ancient sites, and through meditation, ritual and spontaneous dreams.

Other Druidesses prefer to seek out established historical roots, however shadowy, on which to base their spiritual practice. This is quite difficult. I have found as I have researched the history of early Druidry, the Celtic world and the revival of the faith that there are conflicting accounts among historians and researchers which at the present time cannot be resolved.

Because this is essentially a practical workbook, I have provided only a brief overview of these theories here, and have suggested books that you can refer to if you want to study them in depth from different perspectives.

The Roman writer Pliny the Elder, who lived during the first century AD, believed that the word Druid came from the Greek root *drus* or *drous*, the oak. *Wid, vid*, in Sanskrit is to know or see. He or she who has the wisdom or knowledge of the oak was said to have the power to control the elements, so it is a title of power and responsibility. The Welsh for Druid is *derwydd* and the Irish *drao*.

Who Were the Celts?

We know more about the origins of the Celts, whose priests and priestesses, judges, advisers and seers the Druids and Druidesses indisputably were. However, even here there is controversy and uncertainty. Although there is a root Celtic culture and language, there is not a single Celtic race.

The traditional view of historians is still that the ancestors of the Celts were the Proto-Indo Europeans who lived near the Black Sea in around 4000 BC. Then, two waves of Iron Age Celts spread throughout Central Europe: the first was known as the Hallstat culture of 800–500 BC and the second as the La Tene culture of 500–100 BC.

Those who follow this theory state that the Celts colonised Britain and much of the rest of Europe, undergoing great changes as they came into contact with both indigenous cultures and those on their extensive trade routes. By the first century AD, however, the Romans had overcome most of the Celtic tribes and destroyed the centres of Druidry.

The Destruction of Druidry

In AD 48 the Emperor Claudius, who invaded Britain in AD 43, ordered the suppression of Druidry throughout the Celtic lands.

As the Romans gradually conquered Britain, many Druids retreated to Ynys Mon, the Isle of Anglesey, one of their most sacred centres. In AD 60, the Roman military governor of Britain, Suetonius Paulinus, led two legions into north-west Wales and attacked Anglesey.

The Roman historian Tacitus (circa AD 55–117) who, though critical of contemporary Rome, regarded the Celts as savages, described the Druidesses on the banks of Ynys Mon, running, screaming curses in their black robes, their hair in disarray, bearing torches, and the Druids, their hands lifted to the skies, calling down divine aid; these priestesses and priests terrified the Roman soldiers on the opposing bank, 'as if their limbs were paralysed'. But eventually the greater numbers and organisation of the Roman legions prevailed and they destroyed the sacred groves, massacring not only the Druids and Druidesses, but also their children.

The Revival of Druidry

It has been conjectured that the surviving Druids and Druidesses fled to Ireland, Wales, Scotland and Brittany to join Druids and Druidesses who lived there and were, during the ensuing centuries, either converted to Celtic Christianity or died out. Some are said to have used their bardic skills to work as court or travelling minstrels.

Then there is officially verified silence until the mid-thirteenth century, when it has been claimed by modern Druid organisations that that a Druidic group, known as the Mount Haemus Grove, was created at Oxford.

Modern Druidry seems to have come into existence towards the end of the seventeenth century. William Stukeley (1629–97), a scholar and historian who studied Stonehenge and other megaliths, is credited with reviving or creating the Mount Haemus Grove in 1694. His friend and pupil John Toland (1670–1722) began the London Druidic movement that is claimed as a source by a number of modern groups, although some do seek descent back to the Celts.

A meeting was certainly held in 1717 at the Apple Tree Tavern in Covent Garden and Toland was elected as chief of the new order. He then inaugurated the movement with a ceremony on Primrose Hill in London. This is usually taken as the official beginning of modern Druidry, which is why a number of writers, myself included, refer to the eighteenth century as the age of the revival.

A most influential figure, and the one who did most to re-establish claims of Celtic Druidry, is Iolo Morganwg, or Edward Williams (1747–1826). He studied with one of the last authentic Welsh bards of the old tradition and claimed to have possession of an ancient book, the *Barddas*, which contained the ceremonies and beliefs of the ancient Celtic Druids of Wales.

This book was discredited. Some of the material may have been genuinely sourced, but Iolo felt that he needed, like many other scholars of the past, to claim antiquity for the work to have it taken seriously. However, he held the first British Bardic Assembly in 1792 on Primrose Hill, London, and this has been regarded as a landmark in restoring the Celtic Druidic tradition. The Druidry that developed during this period was largely a male, upper middle-class intellectual version that was influenced by Freemasonry in England, whose members wanted a native-based mystical spirituality to give new focus and authenticity to their movement.

The rising fascination in Celtic literature, especially its medieval forms, and a love of all things ancient, also encouraged an interest in Druidry.

Other authorities state that the earliest revived true Druidic order was the masonically influenced Ancient Order of Druids founded in 1781 by Henry Hurle. By 1839, disputes led to the breakaway United Order of Druids, whose traditions spread to the United States and Australia. The latter is now primarily an international and very effective charitable movement. The Ancient Order of Druids, however, developed the spiritual and mystical aspects of Druidry, its most famous member being Winston Churchill. Churchill was a man fascinated by the past and by spiritual traditions. Further splintering occurred when in 1964 Ross Nichols formed the Order of Bards, Ovates and Druids.

Modern Female Druidry

Given that society was, from late Celtic times until the 1960s, patriarchal and class ridden, it is not surprising that Druidry has become female friendly only during the last forty years, although some Druidesses, myself included, find that some of the more formal ceremonies still have a heraldic and stylised format, and officers with formal titles such as the Pendragon can sometimes detract from the simpler folk Druidry we crave. Women have at last become important in the movement, and at the present time Emma Restall Orr is joint chief of the British Order of Druids. The Order of Bards, Ovates and Druids also has women in key positions.

It is estimated that there are around thirty-five formal Druidic organisations in the UK and a number of less formal organisations, and up to two hundred more throughout the world. Some, like the Order of Bards, Ovates and Druids, have an international membership.

Further Reading

Druidry

Some of the older books can be tracked down through bookshops and on the Internet. Seek them out as they are well worth reading.

BONWICK, James, *Irish Druids and Old Irish Religions*, Dorset Press, 1986

CARR-GOMM, Philip, *The Elements of the Druid Tradition*, Element Books, 1996

ELLIS, Peter Berresford, *The Druids*, Constable, 1995

GREEN, Miranda J., *Exploring the World of the Druids*, Thames & Hudson, 1997

MATTHEWS, John, *The Druid Source Book*, Blandford, 1997

NICHOLS, Ross, *The Book of Druidry*, HarperCollins, 1992

PIGGOT, Stuart, *The Druids*, Thames & Hudson, 1985

RESTALL ORR, Emma, *Druid Priestess*, Thorsons, 2001

RESTALL ORR, Emma, *Principles of Druidry*, Thorsons, 1998

Celtic Wisdom, History and Mythology

CONWAY, D. J., *Celtic Magic*, Llewellyn Publications, St Paul, MN, 1995

EASON, Cassandra, *The Complete Guide to Fairies and Magical Beings*, Piatkus, 2001

GRAVES, Robert, *The White Goddess*, Faber & Faber, 1961
GREEN, Miranda J., *Dictionary of Celtic Myth and Legend*, Thames & Hudson, 1992
MATTHEWS, John and Caitlin, *The Encyclopedia of Celtic Wisdom*, Element, 1997
MATTHEWS, John, *Taliesin: Shamanism and the Bardic Mysteries in Britain and Ireland*, Thorsons, 1991
ROSS, Anne, *Pagan Celtic Britain*, Routledge & Kegan Paul, 1967
SPENCE, Lewis, *The Magic Arts in Celtic Britain*, Constable, 1995
STEWART, R. J., *Celtic Myths, Celtic Legends*, Blandford Books, 1997

Herbalism

CRUDEN, Loren, *Medicine Grove, A Shamanic Herbal*, Inner Traditions, 1997
CULPEPER, Nicholas, *Complete Herbal*, Foulsham, 1994
CUNNINGHAM, Scott, *Encyclopedia of Magical Herbs*, Llewellyn Publications, St Paul, MN, 1987
HAWKEY, Sue, *Herbalism*, Southwater Press, 2000
LIPP, Frank J., *Living Wisdom: Herbalism*, Pan, 1996
MABEY, Richard, *The Complete New Herbal*, Penguin, 1991
MILLS, Simon, *The Dictionary of Modern Herbalism*, MJF Books, 1997
VICKERY, Roy, *A Dictionary of Plant Lore*, Oxford University Press, 1995

Oils and Incenses/Smudge

CUNNINGHAM, Scott, *Complete Book of Oils, Incenses and Brews*, Llewellyn Publications, St Paul, MN, 1991
EASON, Cassandra, *Smudging and Incense Burning*, Quantum Essentials, 2001
PRICE, Shirley, *Practical Aromatherapy*, Thorsons, 1996
TISSERAND, Maggie, *Aromatherapy for Women*, Thorsons, 1995
WORWOOD, Valerie Ann, *The Fragrant Pharmacy*, Bantam, 1996
WORWOOD, Valerie Ann, *The Fragrant Heavens*, Doubleday, 1999

Women's Wisdom

EASON, Cassandra, *The Complete Book of Women's Wisdom*, Piatkus, 2001

WALKER, Barbara, *The Woman's Encyclopedia of Myths and Secrets*, Harper Row, 1983

Resources

Druid Organisations

Where there is an active website or email address I have included it.

UK

Central organisation
The Council of British Druid Orders, Elizabeth Murray, 76 Antrobus Road, London W4 5NQ, England
Fosters communication between different groups in the UK and beyond.

The British Druid Order
Joint chiefs: Philip Shallcrass and Emma Restall Orr
PO Box 29, St Leonards-on-Sea, East Sussex TN37 7YP, England
Website: www.druidorder.co.uk
Email addresses: greywolf@druidorder.demon.co.uk
bobcat@nemeton.demon.co.uk
Recreates native British spirituality; open, accessible rituals; pagan and Goddess orientated, but welcomes all.

The Glastonbury Order of Druids
R. Maughfling and J. Paterson, Dove House, Barton-St David, Somerset TA11 6DF, England
Works within the mystical tradition of Glastonbury.

The London Druid Group
Gordon Gentry, 74 Riversmeet, Hertford SG14 1LE, England
Celtic and magical connections.

The Order of Bards, Ovates and Druids
Chosen chief: Philip Carr-Gomm
OBOD, Dept IBWS, PO Box 1333, Lewes, East Sussex BN7
1DX, England
Website: www.obod.co.uk
Email address: office@obod.co.uk
Both Christian and pagan members, welcomes all.
The Order of Bards, Ovates and Druids has a three-year plus
correspondence course, with good tutorial system and groups
throughout the world, including the Netherlands, America and
Australia.

Ireland

The Druid Clan of Dana, an offshoot of the international
Goddess organisation of the Fellowship of Isis
Contact through Fellowship of Isis, PO Box 19152, Tucson, AZ
85751 or Lady Olivia Robertson at Clonegal Castle, Enniscorthy,
Eire
On-line information from the Queensland, Australian Boann and
Dagda Grove Gobann.filid@yahoo.com
Also in Germany www.druid-clan-of-dana.de
In America try the page of the Archdruidess Mara Freeman at
www.chalicecenter.com
The best of Goddess reverence and Celtic Druidry. Organises
courses.

USA

The Henge of Keltria
President: David Schaal, email: DSchaal@aol.com
Keltria, Dept IBWS, PO Box 48369, Minneapolis, MN, USA
55448
Email address: Tony Taylor at keltria@aol.com
Neopagan Celtic Druid organisation.

The United Ancient Order of Druids
Contact the Ional grove via Jeff Davis, Hwy #1521, Dept IBWS,
Arlington, VA, USA 22202-3818
Email the secretary: paulb@cpcug.org
Fraternal Druids.

Ar nDraiocht Fein
Former Archdruid Emeritus is Isaac Bonewits. His own website is
brilliant: bonewits@neopagan.net
Email address: New Archdruid John Adelmann at
adf-archdruid@adf.org
The group emphasises scholarship and aims to recreate authentic
paganism, based on Baltic, Celtic, Germanic, Slavic and early
Greek and Roman beliefs.

Canada

Druiidica Comardia Eriutalamonos (Druidical Fellowship of the
Western Land)
M. G. Boutet, 32 Fourth Ave. South, Roxboro, PQ, H2I 3W3,
Canada

Druidic Healing Organisations

Worldwide

The Druidic College of Healing; contact Dr Kennan Elkman,
PO Box 1414, Albany, WA 6331 Australia
Email address: elkman@healthquest.com.au
List of practitioners; also the College of Traditional Medicine Ways
with an excellent ten-week foundation course and two-year
diploma course.

On-line Druidry

Alt.religion.druid

Tree Conservation/Woodland Burial Sites

This list is not exhaustive.

UK

AB Wildlife Trust Fund
John Bradfield, 7 Knox Road, North Yorkshire HG1 3HF, England
Burials with wildlife and trees.

The British Trust for Conservation Volunteers
Public Relations Officer, 26 St Mary's Street, Wallingford, Oxon
OX10 0EU, England
Aims to restore indigenous woodlands; can dedicate a tree to a
loved one.

Forestry Commission
Department of Forestry, Corstorphine Road, Edinburgh EH12
7AT, Scotland
Will consider woodland memorials; constant replanting schemes;
rents out chalets in forests all over Britain.

Sherwood Forest Initiative
Project Director, Cuckney Road, Carburton, Worksop, Notts S80
3BP, England
Restoring the forest; woodland memorials.

Woodland Creations
Tim and Nicky Reed, The Guildhouse, Tredethick, Lostithiel,
Cornwall PL22 0LE, England
Dedicated to restoring native woodlands to Cornwall.

Flower/Tree Essences, Suppliers and Courses

UK

Bach Flower Remedies
Healing Herbs Ltd, PO Box 65, Hereford HR2 0UW, England

USA and Canada

Alaskan Flower Essence Project
PO Box 1329, Homer AL 99603, USA

USA

Desert Alchemy
PO Box 44189, Tucson, AZ 85733, USA

Canada

Pacific Essences
PO Box 8317, Victoria, V8W 3R9, Canada

Australia

The Australian Tree Essences
Contact Sabian, PO Box 527, Kew, Victoria, Australia 3101 or The
Sabian Centre, 11 Selbourne Road, Kew, Victoria, Australia 3101

Index

Page numbers in *italics* refer to diagrams, page numbers in **bold** refer to information presented in tables.

Aengus/Oengus Og 161
agrimony 130
Aine 61, 157, 161
Air 42
    guardian of 52
    properties of 45–6
    and the Three Realm ritual 57, 58
    and triple circle casting 44
    and weaving the elements 49
Airmid 123
Alban 172
Alban Arthuran (the Light of Arthur) 174–6
    see also Midwinter Solstice
Alban Eiler 177–8
    see also Spring Equinox
Alban Elued 182–4
    see also Autumn Equinox
Alban Heruin (the Light of the Shore) 180–1
    see also Midsummer Solstice
alder 27, 110
Alder Mother 110
almond 27
Amiens Cathedral, Picardy, France 72
Ana/Anu 80, 161
Ancient Order of Druids 198

angelica 130
Anglesey, Isle of (Ynys Mon) 196
animals
    animal cards 146–7, 167
    attraction to sacred groves 13
    shapeshifting 138–47
anise/aniseed 130
Annwyn (Otherworld) 65
Aoife 16
Aper 4
apple 27, 114
Apple Mother 114
Arduinna 80, 161–2, 167
Arianrhod 46, 53, 80, 162, 188
art 14
ash 27, 111
Ash Mother 111
aspen 27
Aum (Buddhist chant) 64, 65
auras 21, 139, 140–1
Australia 198
Autumn Equinox 7, 182–4
Avebury Stones, Wiltshire 170–1, 189
avocado 27
Awen 64–70
    chant 64–5, 67, 171
    'Opening the Doorway' ritual 68–70

Awen – *contd*
  symbol 65–6, *65*, 267
  using the inspiration of 68
  working with 66–7

Badhbh/Nemhain 162
Balor 92–3
bamboo 27
banana 27
banyan 27
Bards 14, 33, 192
  see also Taliesin
barrows 100, 101
basil 130
bay 27–8, 130–1
bears 142
beech 28
Bel, Belenus, Beli, Belinus,
    Belenos, Bile 47, 162
Belisama/Belili 162
Beltaine Fire 179–80
Beltaine/Beltane (May Day) 173,
    179–80
birch 28, 109
Birch Mother 109
birds 139–40, 142, 143, 144, 145
bistort 131
blackbirds 139–40, 142, 167
blackthorn 116
Blackthorn Mother 116
bladderwrack 133
Blodeuwedd, Bloddeudd, Blodwin,
    Blanchefour 80, 162
Boann/Boanne 157, 162
boars 142
Book of the Dun Cow 157
Boudicca 54
boxwood 28
bracken 115–16
Bran the Blessed 162
Branwen 162–3
Brighid 47, 61, 66, 123, 163, 176,
    188, 189

Britain 1, 196
British Bardic Assembly 197
British Druid Order 33, 185, 202
British Museum 58
bulls 143
burial grounds 100, 101, 148

Cad Goddeu (The Battle of the
    Trees) (Celtic poem) 103, 109
Caesar, Julius 77, 153
Cailleach 45, 163
Caillos 78
calendars
  Celtic 76–7
  lunar 75–6, 77–80
Canada 189
candles 35, 36–7
cards
  animal 146–7, 167
  deity 167
  tree 26
cauldrons 120, 124, 126
caves 101–2
cedar 28
Celtic New Year 173
Celts 1–2, 191, 195
  calendar of 76–7
  deities of 61, 76, 120, 123, 124,
      149, 156–67
  and the four elements 42
  healing Goddesses of 120, 123,
      124
  herbalism of 121
  and land wights 55
  and the Moon 75
  oral tradition of 17
  origins of 196
  power animals of 139–40,
      142–5
  seers of 92
  and Sun Mothers 61
  Sun times of 73
  and the Three Realms 43

and trees 20, 26, 103, 104, 105, 106, 109–19
and the Triple Goddess 76
and triskeles 58
and the west 53
Cernunnos/Hern the Hunter 45, 156, 159, 163
Cerridwen 47, 66, 67, 80, 123, 138–9, 159, 163, 188
chakras 22
chamomile, Roman/German 131
cherry 28
chestnut 28
Christianity 2, 71–2, 121, 168, 197
Churchill, Winston 198
Cian 92
Claudius 196
cleansing herbs 123–4, 125, 126
Cliodhna of the Golden Hair 163
cloud divination 95–8
coconut 28
Coligny calendar 77–8
college of nine priestesses 188–90
corn dollies 182
counselling 92–9
Coventina 163
cows 143
crane bags 16–17
cranes 143
crystals
    for dedicating sacred groves 34, 35
    pendulums 24, 26
    and the Sun 72
    and Tree Mothers 108
cultures, root 153–5
cypress 28

Dagda, The 163–4
Dana/Danu 161, 164
dandelion 131
darkness 76–7

date palm 31
dawn 71–2
death 193
decoctions 129
deer 143
defining Druidry 1–2
deities 45, 46, 47–8
    see also specific deities
    balancing the good and evil in 158–9
    choosing 166–7
    deity cards 167
    deity focuses 160
    finding 159–60
    healing goddesses 120, 123, 124
    modern relevance of Celtic 157–8
    offerings for 160–1
    representations of 159
    sources of knowledge on 156–7
    typology of 161–6
    working with Celtic 156–67
destruction of Druidry 196
Diancecht 123
diet 169
Dinton Pastures Country Park 12
Diocletian 4, 92
distance healing 122–3, 124, 126–7
divination 90–102
    by clouds 95–8
    by fire 94–5
    by trees 108
    by water 98–9
    counselling skills for 92–9
    developing prophetic powers 100–2
    and interpreting nature's wisdom 90–1
    personal symbol systems for 91–2
    tools of natural 94
    wise use of 93–4

dogs 143
dogwood 28
Donn 164
dragons 143
Druantia 104, 164, 188
dusk 73

eagles 143
Earth 42
    guardian of 52
    properties of 45
    and triple circle casting 43–4
    and triskeles 60
    and weaving the elements
        49–50
Earth Mother 66, 76, 87, 127,
    176
Earth, realm of 54–5
    and Awen 66
    and healing 127
    in ritual 57–8
    and triple circle casting 43–4
    and triskeles 60
eclipses, solar 62
Eden Project, Cornwall 25
elder 28–9, 116
Elder Mother 38, 104, 116–17
electromagnetic fields 169
elemental guardians 52–3
elm 29
emails 65
energy vibrations 21, 22–3
    see also auras
England 127
English Heritage 189
environmental awareness 185–6
ephemeris 87
Epona 164
equinox water 178
equinoxes 70–1, 72, 171–2, 173
    Autumn 7, 182–4
    and Awen 65
    Spring 72, 149, 177–8

equipment 13–18, 124
Eriu 164
essences, tree 25
Ethiniu 80
Ethniu 92
eucalyptus 29
evil 158–9
exercises
    using Awen 66–7, 68–70
    casting sacred circles 44
    cloud divination 96–8
    connecting with your ancestors
        151–3
    dedicating sacred groves 34–7
    finding your root culture 153–5
    fire divination 95
    grounding yourself 23–4
    healing 124–7
    making sun water 62–3
    merging with the essence of a
        tree 22–3
    mistletoe rites 85–6
    Moon rituals 81–3, 85–6
    rebirth rituals 149–50
    shapeshifting 140–2, 146–7
    three Realms 57–8
    water divination 98–9
eye of the Sun 61
eyebright 131–2

fennel 132
fenugreek 132
fern 115
Fern Mother 115–16
fertility rituals 178
Festivals of Light 172–3
feverfew 132
fig 29
Fir Mother 117
fir trees 29, 117
Fire 42, 56, 57
    divination by 94–5
    guardian of 52

properties of 46–7
and triple circle casting 43–4
and weaving the elements 49, 50
Fire/Sun Goddesses 61, 66, 67
flotation tanks 101
formal Orders 5, 7, 33, 185–6, 190–3
    addresses 202–4
    dangerous 191
    finding time for 192
    Revivalist 197–8
    structure of 192–3
forms of Druidry 186–93
fossils 16–17
four elements 42–8
    see also Air; Earth; Fire; Water
    properties of 44–8
    walking the directions 48–50
France 1, 4, 6, 77, 127, 197
    see also Gaul/Gauls
Freemasonry 197–8

Gatekeepers 51
Gaul/Gauls 4, 77, 104
Glastonbury Tor 190
Goddesses, healing 120, 123, 124
Golden Dawn 42
goodness 158–9
gorse 117
Gorse Mother 117–18
Grainne 61, 164
Graves, Robert 103, 108–9
Green Man, The 164–5
grounding 23–4
guardians
    elemental 52–3
    of the night 74
    of sacred groves 37–8
Guest, Lady Charlotte 157
Gwion 138–9
Gwydion 165

Halloween *see* Samhain

Hallstat culture 196
hawks 143
hawthorn 29, 111
Hawthorn Mother 112
hazel 29, 113
Hazel Mother 113
healing
    becoming a healer 120–1
    distant 122–3, 124, 126–7
    herbal 120–37
    sending 126–7
    with sun water 63–4
heather 118
Heather Mother 118
herbs
    choosing 127–37
    cleansing-variety 123–4, 125, 126
    healing 120–37
    to avoid during pregnancy 129–30
    and Tree Mothers 108
    for water divination 99
Herne the Hunter *see* Cernunnos
Hildegard von Bingen 22
Historia Augusta (emperor's biographies) 4
holidays 12
holly 29, 113
Holly Mother 113
honeysuckle 132
horse chestnut 28
horses 143–4
hounds 143
Hurle, Henry 198

Imbolc/Oimelc 176–7
informal groups 187–90
infusions 128–9
initiation 33
inspiration 68–70
Internet 65, 77, 151, 155, 185, 189, 204

Ireland 2, 16, 61, 77, 100, 103, 121, 148, 149, 157, 197
Isle of Man 157
ivy 26, 29–30, 115
Ivy Mother 115

journals 17–18, 91, 187
Jung, Carl Gustav 42
juniper 30, 133

kelp 133
Keltria Order 84–5, 87
Knowth stones, Newgrange, Ireland 77

La Roche 14
La Tene culture 196
land wights 55
lapwings 144
larch 30
laurel 30
lavender 133
ley lines 21
light
    and darkness 76–7
    festivals of 172–3
linden 30
living temples *see* sacred groves
Llew 165
Lugh 92, 165
Lughnassadh 181–2
lunar calendar 75–6, 77–80

Mabinogion (collection of Celtic myths) 157
Mabon 165
Macha/Nass 165
mango 30
Mannanann mac Lir 16, 47, 165
maple 30
marigold 133
marjoram, sweet 134
Matthews, Caitlin 17

Matthews, John 17
May Day *see* Beltaine/Beltane
meadowsweet 134
Mela, Pomponius 4, 138
menstrual cycle 88
Miach 123
midnight 73–4
Midsummer Solstice (Longest Day) 7, 62, 180–1
    and Awen 65, *65*
    and dawn 71–2
    and mistletoe rites 84
    and rebirth rituals 149
Midwinter Full Moon 75
Midwinter Solstice 62, 174–6
    and Awen 65, *65*
    and dawn 71–2
    and developing prophetic power 100
    and midnight 73
    and rebirth rituals 148, 149, 150
mint, water 134
mistletoe 26, 30
    healing properties 85, 86, 127
    poisonous properties 127
    rites 84–6
Modron 166
Mont St-Michel, France 4
months, lunar 77–80
moods, lunar influences on 88
Moon 3, 61
    blue 79
    calendar of the 75–6, 77–80
    Full 75, 76, 77, 78–83, 87, 88–9
    and mistletoe rites 84–6
    New 85–7
    phases of 12, 87–9
    rituals 79–89, **79–80**
    sixth day of 84–6
    waning 87, 89
    waxing (Crescent) 87, 88
    working with the 75–89

Moon Mother 75, 80, 83
Moon water 82–3
Morgan le Fey/Morgana 166
Morganwg, Iolo (Edward
    Williams) 197
mortar and pestle 124
Mother Goddess 165, 177–8
Mount Haemus Grove 197
mountain ash *see* rowan
mugwort 134
myrtle 30

names, of power 18
National Trust 189–90
nature, wisdom of 90–1
Nectan 157
Nemetona/Nemain 104, 166
nettle 135
New Forest 11–12
New Moon rites 86–7
New Year, Celtic 173
New Year's Day 149
Newgrange, Boyne Valley, Ireland
    77, 148, 149
Nichols, Ross 198
'nine Druidesses' stories 4, 6
nine priestesses, college of 188–90
noon 72
Norfolk Island pine 30–1
Numerian 4

oak 20, 21, 31, 112
Oak Mother 112
offerings 160–1
O'Flaherty 103
Ogma 103
oils
    Sun 181
    tree 25
olive 31
'Opening the Doorway' ritual
    68–70
oracle cards 26

oracles 90–102
oral tradition 17, 157, 195
orange 31
Order of Bards, Ovates and
    Druids (OBOD) 7, 170,
    191, 198, 203
origins of Druidry 3–4, 195
Orkney Islands 104
Orr, Emma Restall 18, 138, 198
otters 144
Ovates 14, 192
owls 144

pagan festivals 168
palm, date 31
parsley 135
passage graves 148
past lives 153
patriarchal organisations 191, 198
Paulinus, Suetonius 196
peach 31
pear 31
pendulums, crystal 24, 26
Pentre Ifan cromlech, Wales 4
peppermint 134
pine 30–1, 117
Plato 42
Pliny the Elder 20, 77, 84, 127,
    195
poplar, black and white 31, 118
Poplar Mother 118–19
power names 18
pregnancy, herbs to avoid during
    129–30
prophecy *see* divination
Proto-Indo Europeans 196
psychotherapy 42

rebirth ritual 149–50
redwood 32
responsibilities of Druidesses 9
Revivalist Druidry 191
    and Awen 65–6

Revivalist Druidry – *contd*
  developing prophetic powers for
      100
  and the four elements 42
  history of 197–8
  and triskeles 58
  women in 5
Rhiannon 80, 139, 166, 167
rituals 18–19
  for Alban Arthuran 174–5
  for Alban Eiler 177
  for Alban Elued 183
  for Alban Heruin 180
  for Beltaine 179
  for cloud divination 96–8
  for developing personal
      prophetic powers 100, 101
  for fire divination 95
  for herbal healing 124–7
  using herbs in 128–9
  for Imbolc/Oimelc 176
  for Lughnassadh 181–2
  Moon 79–89, **79–80**
  for 'Opening the Doorway'
      68–70
  preparing for 50
  for rebirth 149–50
  and sacred circles 50–4
  for Samhain 173
  Three Realms in 5708
  for water divination 98–9
robes 14–15
Rollright Stones, Oxfordshire 104
Romans 2, 4, 17, 54, 76, 77, 156,
      159, 196
rose 135
rose absolute 135
rose Otto 135
rosemary 135–6
rowan 32, 100, 109
Rowan Mother 109–10

sacred circles 40–60

  casting elemental 43–8
  casting for groups 43
  centres of 51
  and elemental guardians 52–3
  and the four elements 42–8
  power of 41
  and rituals 50–4
  and the Three Realms 54–8
  triple 43–4
  and triskeles 58–60
  walking the directions 48–50
  and the Wise Ancestors 53–4
  for working outside sacred
      groves 41–2
sacred groves 10–13, 20–39
  dedicating 33–7
  grounding yourself in 23–4
  guardians of 37–8
  setting up 12–13
  and tree oracle cards 26
  and tree symbolism 26–33
  understanding and recognising
      trees 21–3
  use in the everyday world 38–9
  visualising 24–6
sacred sites 189–90
sage 136
St John's wort 136
salmon 144
Samhain (Halloween) 8–9, 173–4
santons 175–6
Scotland 103, 157, 197
scrying 92, 98–9
Sea, realm of 55–6
  and Awen 66
  and healing 127
  in ritual 58
  and triple circle casting 43–4
  and triskeles 60
seasonal affective disorder (SAD)
      169–70
seasons 12, 70–1, 168–84
Sena, island of 4, 138

serpents/snakes 144
shapeshifting 138–47
   animal forms 142–5
   choosing a power creature 145–7
   technique 140–2
Shining Ones 50, 51
silver banksia 32
Sky, realm of 56
   and Awen 66
   and healing 127
   and Moon rituals 82
   in ritual 58
   and triple circle casting 43–4
   and triskeles 60
smudge sticks 16, 35, 36–7, 44
solar eclipses 62
solitary practitioners 186–7
solstice water 181
solstices 70–1, 171–2, 173
   see also Midsummer Solstice;
      Midwinter Solstice
sows 144
spiritual herbalism 122–7
spirituality, universal 2–3
Spring Equinox 72, 149, 177–8
staffs 15–16, 81
stags 144
Stonehenge 189
Strabo 192
Stukeley, William 197
Sulis 61
Sun 2
   and Awen 64–70
   female power of 61–2
   herbs of 69, 70
   oils/incenses of 181
   seasons of 70–1
   times of 71–4
   water of 62–4, 69, 70
   working with 61–74
Sun, eye of the 61
Sun Mothers 61
Sun wheel gardens 181

Sun/Fire Goddesses 61, 66, 67
swans 144
sycamore 32
symbolism
   personal 91–2
   for staffs 15–16
   of the Tree Mothers 108,
      109–19
   of trees 26–33

Tacitus 196
Taliesin 103, 139, 153
tamarind 32
Taranis 46, 156, 159, 166
tarragon 136
Three Realms 43–4, 54–8, 66
   see also Earth, realm of; Sea,
      realm of; Sky, realm of
thyme 136–7
Toland, John 197
training 1, 191
tree alphabet 103–4
Tree Grandmothers 105
Tree Mothers 20, 35, 38
   becoming 103–19
   identifying 105–6
   messages of 108–9
   symbols of 108, 109–19
   typology of 109–19
tree oracle cards 26
trees 10–12, 20–6
   becoming tree-wise 106–7
   and the dedication of sacred
      groves 33–7
   divination by 108
   essences/oils 25
   listening to the leaves of 107–8
   merging with the essence/spirit
      of 22–3
   symbolism of 26–33
   understanding and
      21–3
   visualising 24–6

triple circles 43–4
Triple Goddess 76
triskeles 58–60, *59*

United Order of Druids 198
United States 189, 198
universal spirituality 2–3

Vates 192
veriditas 22
vervain 87, 137
vine 26, 32, 114
Vine Mother 114–15
visualisation 24–6

Wales 4, 157
walnut 32
water
    equinox-type 178
    Moon 82–3
    solstice-type 181
    sources 12, 34, 36
    Sun 62–4, 69, 70
water divination (scrying) 92,
        98–9
Water (element) 42, 44, 49–50
    guardian of 52
    properties of 47–8
weather 12
Wellington Country Park, nr
        Basingstoke 12

Wheel of the Year 70–1, 167, 169,
        171–84, *172*
White Goddess, trees of 28–9, 32
white mangrove 32–3
Williams, Edward 197
willow 32, 110
Willow Mother 110–11
wisdom, of nature 90–1
Wise Ancestors 53–4, 59, 90,
        193
    finding your ancestors 151–3
    finding your root culture 153–5
    and midnight 74
    and the rebirth ritual 149–50
    time of (Samhain) 173
    working with 148–55
witchcraft 18–19, 40–1, 50–1, 54,
        76, 173
    Druidesses who practise 41
wolves 144–5
women
    and Druidry 3
    and the Moon 75
    as natural healers 120
    and sacred circles 41
    and trees 20–1
wrens 145

year, Druidic 70–1, 168–84
yew 33, 119
Yew Mother 119

Other titles by Cassandra Eason

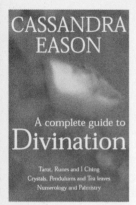

CASSANDRA EASON

A complete guide to
Divination

Tarot, Runes and I Ching
Crystals, Pendulums and Tea leaves
Numerology and Palmistry

0 7499 2304 0   £7.99 PB

A complete guide to
**FAIRIES &
MAGICAL
BEINGS**

CASSANDRA EASON

0 7499 2162 5   £9.99 PB

CASSANDRA EASON

A complete guide to
**Night
Magic**

Moon and Star Magic
Angels, Fairies and Animals of the Night
Candles, Meditations and Healing

0 7499 2361 X   £9.99 PB

CASSANDRA EASON

A complete
guide to
**Magic
and Ritual**

Spells, Rituals and Chants
Auras, Spirits and Angels
Folklore, Herbs and Crystals

0 7499 2311 3   £7.99 PB

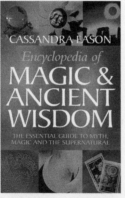

CASSANDRA EASON
Encyclopedia of
**MAGIC &
ANCIENT
WISDOM**

THE ESSENTIAL GUIDE TO MYTH,
MAGIC AND THE SUPERNATURAL

0 7499 2240 0   £12.99 PB

CASSANDRA
EASON

10 Steps to
**Psychic
Power**

Intuition, Meditation and Magic
Auras, Chakras, Healing and Protection
Earth Spirits, Ghosts, Guides and Angels

0 7499 2293 1   £12.99 PB

CASSANDRA
EASON

A complete guide to
**Psychic
Development**

Visualisation and Magic
Auras, Chakras and Healing
Channelling, Guides and Angels

0 7499 2323 7   £7.99 PB

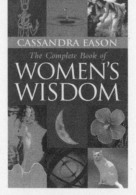

CASSANDRA EASON
The Complete Book of
**WOMEN'S
WISDOM**

0 7499 2209 5   £17.99 HB